FROM RETREAT TO DEFEAT

THE LAST YEARS OF THE GERMAN ARMY ON THE EASTERN FRONT 1943–45

A Photographic History

Ian Baxter

Helion & Company Ltd

Helion & Company Limited
26 Willow Road
Solihull
West Midlands
B91 1UE
England
Tel. 0121 705 3393
Fax 0121 711 4075
Email: publishing@helion.co.uk
Website: http://www.helion.co.uk

Published by Helion & Company 2007

Designed and typeset by Helion & Company Limited, Solihull, West Midlands
Cover designed by Bookcraft Limited, Stroud, Gloucestershire
Printed by Cromwell Press Ltd, Trowbridge, Wiltshire

Text © Ian Baxter 2006
Photographs © HITM Photo Archive (www.hitm-archive.co.uk), Ullstein Bilderdienst (Ullstein)
Maps © Helion & Company Ltd

Front cover images: top – A MG34 machine gunner standing inside the cupola of his tank during the winter of 1943/44 (HITM), bottom – a pensive-looking group of German grenadiers awaiting orders to begin a counter-attack, in the Kurland pocket, February 1945 (Ullstein Bilderdienst).
Rear cover image: A rapid command conference in the field, July 1944. The commander of a Sturmgeschütz unit gives orders to his men – the strain of combat is clearly visible. (Ullstein Bilderdienst).

ISBN 978 1 906033 01 9

British Library Cataloguing-in-Publication Data.
A catalogue record for this book is available from the British Library.

All rights reserved. No part of this publication may be reproduced, stored in a retrieval system, or transmitted, in any form, or by any means, electronic, mechanical, photocopying, recording or otherwise, without the express written consent of Helion & Company Limited.

For details of other military history titles published by Helion & Company Limited contact the above address, or visit our website: http://www.helion.co.uk.

We always welcome receiving book proposals from prospective authors.

Contents

Photographic acknowledgements. iv
Introduction v

Prologue: Prelude to disaster, the German soldier in Russia 1941–43 6

Part I: Summer 1943–Winter 1943/44
1   Kursk 9
2   Fighting withdrawal. 31

Part II: Winter 1943/44–Autumn 1944
3   Winter warfare 42
4   The destruction of Army Group Centre 63
5   Defending Poland. 75

Part III: Winter 1944/45–May 1945
6   Army in retreat 90
7   Last battles around Berlin 106
8   Berlin falls 119
    Epilogue 130

Appendices
I   Uniforms 131
II   Personal equipment and weapons 133
III   Organisation, unit listings 135
IV   German Order of Battle Eastern Front July 1943 144
V   German Order of Battle Eastern Front 15 June 1944 149
VI   German Order of Battle, Berlin, 12–26 April 1945 153
VII   German Army Ranks 155

    Bibliography. 156

Photographic acknowledgements

It is with the greatest pleasure that I use this opportunity on concluding this book to thank those who helped make this volume possible. My expression of gratitude first goes to my German photographic collector Rolf Halfen. He has been an unfailing source; supplying me with a number of photographs that were obtained from numerous private sources. Throughout the research stage of this book Rolf searched and contacted numerous collectors all over Germany, trying to find a multitude of interesting and rare photographs.

Further afield in Poland I am also extremely grateful to Marcin Kaludow, my Polish photographic specialist, who supplied me with a great variety of photographs that he sourced from private photographic collections in Poland, Russia and the Ukraine.

Finally, I wish to display my kindness and appreciation to my American photographic collector, Richard White, who supplied me with a number of rare unpublished photographs, especially showing the various Luftwaffe field divisions deployed on the Eastern Front.

Introduction

From *Retreat to Defeat: The Last Years of the German Army on the Eastern Front 1943–45* is a unique insight into the last desperate years of the German Army at war. On the vast wastelands of the Soviet Union, the book describes how the German Army together with the elite mountain troops and Luftwaffe field divisions played a decisive role in trying to stem the rout along the disintegrating front lines. Drawing on previously rare and unpublished photographs with in-depth captions, the book provides an absorbing analysis of this traumatic period of the war. It reveals in detail how the beginning of the end began at the battle of Kursk, and how this massive operation led to the Red Army recapturing huge areas of the Soviet Union and bleeding white the German armies it struck. Despite the adverse situation in which the German Army was placed, soldiers were still infused to fight to the bitter end and attempt to build new lines of defence. But as the Red Army launched its long awaited summer offensive, codenamed 'Operation Bagration', this study reveals how the German Army was forced to withdraw under the constant hammer blows of ground and air bombardments. Those German forces that survived the artillery barrages, the onslaught of the tank armadas, and mass infantry assaults, streamed back from the battlefield and fought vicious battles through the Baltic states, Byelorussia, and built up new defences along the Vistula in Poland. As the final months of the war were played out on the Eastern Front it depicts how the German Army, with diminishing resources, withdrew across a devastated Reich and fought out the last battles with party militia forces around a bombed and blasted Berlin.

Prologue

Prelude to Disaster: the German Soldier in Russia 1941–43

At dawn on 22 June 1941, along an 1800-mile long invasion front, three million German soldiers poured across the frontier of the Soviet Union to begin what was known to the German Army as 'Operation Barbarossa', the German invasion of Russia. The German Army divided their forces into three army groups; Army Group North, under the command of Feldmarschall Ritter von Leeb; Army Group Centre, under Feldmarschall Fedor von Bock; and Army Group South, under the Feldmarschall Gerd von Rundstedt. As with the other successful Blitzkrieg campaigns in Poland and France, the Panzer arm were kept separate from the soldiers, and were concentrated in four independent *Gruppen*, under the skilful command of Kleist, Guderian, Hoth, and Hoepner. All three army groups were given the main objective of Leningrad, Moscow, and the Ukraine. The Panzer divisions were to systematically carve up the Red Army whilst the slower moving infantry and artillery were to force their surrender.

For the German soldier that entered Russia that morning they found the first clashes with the enemy very limited. Across the entire invasion front, the Soviet Army had been taken completely by surprise. Everywhere there were scenes of total carnage and devastation. In the north three Panzer divisions and two infantry divisions had a frontage of less than twenty-five miles. In the centre, Bock's group with devastating superiority of numbers and firepower selected their armoured penetration with precision and deadly effect. The soldiers that followed in the wake of this armoured *schwerpunkt* were amazed by the speed. In the south leading elements of all the four German armoured groups were driving almost unhindered along the dry roads. By the evening of 22 June all the leading Panzer divisions were well clear of the fighting zone leaving the infantry to mop up the last remnants of what seemed a defeated enemy army.

For the next few weeks the campaign went like clockwork. By 10 July Bock's troops had penetrated almost to the city of Smolensk. When they reached this city they stood a mere 230 miles from the greatest prize of them all – Moscow. At an average rate of advance of eighteen miles a day an air of confidence spread through the German Army. Many of them soon believed Moscow would soon be reached. In the last weeks of July and early August German forces of Army Group Centre lunged forward into the depth of the Soviet land mass and continued fighting over seemingly endless terrain, through huge forests, over dusty roads, and through the mud and mire when the summer thunderstorms had turned the land into a bottomless bog, which in turn reduced the speed of the advance. But still they continued pushing forward and forcing their way across numerous rivers and streams, and capturing thousands of Russian soldiers either in large direct frontal assaults or vast pincer movements. The endless march to Moscow was a tribute to the German soldier who had to endure such adverse conditions in the face of terrible, often unknown and seemingly difficult terrain against a nation that now despised them. To these soldiers following in the wake of the mighty panzer forces there was a feeling of exhilaration fuelled the prospect of reaching Moscow and finally settling scores with their old arch-enemy.

With victory beckoning Operation Typhoon, the German advance on Moscow, began in earnest during the early hours of 30 September 1941. Within hours of the first lightening strike Bock's forces were surrounding Red Army formations and pouring a storm of fire into the dwindling enemy ranks. In a matter of hours vital Russian sectors were already subsiding like landslides. But in spite of this initial success the German soldier was becoming increasingly uneasy about the fighting. Although the Red Army seemed always to be on the retreat, they were always fighting. Frequently they felt that the Russians were luring them even deeper into the east. Another worry was that the mass of German infantry was finding it difficult to maintain pace with the fast moving armour. Consequently, the bulk of them were now facing fierce resistance. To make problems even worse, by October the weather began to change as cold driving rain and sleet fell on the central front. Within hours the Russian countryside had been turned into a quagmire with roads and fields becoming virtually impassable. All the roads leading to Moscow had become boggy swamps. Although tanks and other tracked wheeled vehicles managed to push through the mire at a slow pace, trucks and other wheeled vehicles were hopelessly stuck up to their axles in deep boggy mud. Despite frantic efforts by thousands of soldiers to pull them free, the progress was painfully slow. Within a month there still seemed no sight of reaching the Red capital. Resistance too had become even worse. In Army Group Centre alone some 35,000 German soldiers had been lost, excluding the sick and wounded. By November worrying concerns were beginning to fester among many of the commanders regarding the lack of winter supplies. They knew that the winter itself would soon create a graver problem than the Russians themselves. But no one in the *Ostheer* had taken into account that Bock's soldiers would be slogging desperately up to their knees in the mud in October and deep snow in November.

Despite the mire that brought virtually the entire central front to a crawl, the weather improved slightly and within a few weeks advanced elements were now within touching distance of Moscow. But yet again weather conditions became much worse. Heavy rain, snow showers, and penetrating mists made movement almost impossible. Slowly the movement of troops and Panzers halted through fatigue, shortages and the climate. The Red Army then took immediate advantage of the situation and attacked them without respite, pulverising their positions with Katyusha rocket mortars. During the first days of November after struggling through mud and minefields, German supply lines had become overstretched, vehicles were breaking down and casualty returns were mounting. Stagnated in front of Moscow Bock ordered that he would have to regroup the entire central front before the final march on the capital. Yet, by mid-November with his soldiers still exhausted and understrength Hitler ordered them to push forward to Moscow and capture it before the first heavy snow blizzards began. Although at first the advance went well, freezing temperatures and fanatical resistance caused them once again to halt. To the south of Moscow Guderian's force also came perilously close to achieving its objective. But the weather hampered any attempt of gaining ground. Instead of driving his men forward into action Guderian was compelled to fight a defensive battle of attrition in terrible arctic conditions. Day by day the ingredients for disaster mounted. Despair now gripped the entire Eastern Front. No more than forty miles from the outskirts of the city advanced elements of Bock's force remained paralysed and unable to avert the situation.

With Moscow saved from German capture, in the north soldiers of Leeb's Army Group North were also unable to attain their objective by capturing the smouldering city of Leningrad. In the south Army Group South had fared much better and had already battered its way through towards Kursk until finally halting in the bottomless mire and snow blizzards. By March 1942 both German and Russian soldiers alike finally accepted defeat by the weather. An enforced true suddenly descended upon the Eastern Front until early May. During this time the German Army tended to its wounds. In an attempt to restore morale among the troops, which had been lost the previous winter, the Army had produced a handbook for the soldier in Russia. The handbook was distributed well before the onset of any more bad weather. The book assured the German soldier that he could meet and overcome the strains and difficulties of campaigning in the East with harsh sub-zero temperatures. Much of the book was concerned with various ways of overcoming freezing weather, which included the construction of shelters, with igloos highly recommended. Pages were devoted to the construction of primitive but effective stoves, the maintenance of vehicles, how to cook food, type of clothing to wear, animal care, the effects of various terrain and how to overcome it, effective camouflage and trench building, running railway lines across a frozen river or lake, and it even contained the effects of climate on the railway network. Drastic efforts were made to convince the German soldier that snow could also serve as an ally not as an element that was feared. Although the book was highly recommended, some soldiers saw it as an omen, believing another winter in Russia was perhaps imminent.

With a new air of confidence, the Germans opened up a new long-awaited offensive in the south, calling it 'Operation Blue' on 8 May 1942. Army Group South was to pinch out the Izyum pocket and enclose Voronezh on the Don in armoured pincers. Once that had been accomplished, Army Group Centre would drive down the Don and across the Steppe to an industrial city called Stalingrad on the Volga, joined by another force advancing from Kharkov. Once this was completed its spearheads would race across the mountain range between the Black and Caspian Seas and reach Baku, the centre of the Soviet oil industry.

Within a week of 'Operation Blue' being unleashed down to the Kerch Peninsula of the Crimea, over 170,000 Russian troops had been taken prisoner. Only Sevastopol, which would not fall until 2 July, still held grimly to its coastal batteries. On 22 May General Kleist, commanding the 1st Panzer Army, joined up with General Paulus' 6. Armee south of Kharkov and achieved another astonishing encirclement. By early June 239,000 prisoners had been captured and 1240 tanks destroyed on the Kharkov battlefield. Meanwhile the 6th Army, supported by the 4th Panzer Army, was to thrust forward toward Stalingrad with the objective of destroying the enemy forces concentrated there, to occupy the city and to block land communications between the Don and Volga.

By late August 1942, after four months of the summer offensive in the south, leading elements of Paulus's 6th Army had reached the banks of the Volga and were preparing to unleash its soldiers against the city of Stalingrad. In spite of the success of 'Operation Blue' the Red Army was still not defeated. Vast areas of Russia too had not been conquered, including the Caucasus. Here in this far distant land every German soldier began to wonder when the war in the East would finally end. To the men trudging eastward, they were over 1,000 miles from Silesia and some 1,500 miles from the Rhineland. Many soldiers began to believe that success of the war lay in the capture of Stalingrad. However, by Christmas 1942 that belief slowly dissipated as the whole of the 6th Army were encircled and systematically annihilated in the ruins of the city. During this critical period, until the 6th Army surrendered in early

February 1943, the Germans and their Allies around Stalingrad gradually ran all their divisions into the ground with fatigue and high casualties.

The first days of 1943 opened as had 1942 with the German Army suffering unimaginable casualties and huge losses of equipment. Nearly six hundred miles of the front had stagnated, with some battles being fought out similar to the conditions in the First World War. From the frozen Baltic, around the city of Leningrad, south to Lake Ilmem, and across the vast tall pine forests of the Rzhev salient, and then down to Orel, German soldiers had hardly moved in twelve bitter months of fighting. Here across this vast sprawling front were thousands of permanent emplacements of logs and earth shelters dug by the soldiers. Hundreds of concrete bunkers had been constructed with enormous mine fields that had been laid during the spring and summer of 1942. Across the desolate terrain that was comparable to the trenches of the Western Front in World War One, the soldiers lived fairly comfortably. They were well clothed, rations were in abundance, there was plenty of fuel, and even mail was delivered to them from home regularly. With often days without fighting, the Germans used these lines as a rest area for worn-out divisions.

Whilst many parts of the front remained stagnated, in the south and in the Ukraine, the campaign was being decided. By February 1943 the front had moved almost two hundred miles in less than three months. As German infantry and their Waffen-SS counterparts withdrew they devastated the whole countryside and razed towns. But despite the German retreat, the Soviets first experience of an offensive was proving more difficult than they first envisaged. As a consequence during the last two weeks of February 1943 a complete dramatic reversal of fortune gripped the German Army, which was later called by the soldiers that fought in it, the 'miracle of the Donetz'. South of Kharkov under converging pressure from General Hoth's two Panzer Corps, the exhausted Russian armies began to disintegrate and retreat in an easterly direction. Within a week German pincers had closed following a meeting between Hoth's forces and the Waffen-SS. However, due to their relatively small numbers German infantry were unable to seal the pocket completely, and many Russian soldiers clawed their way out on foot or on horseback, crossing unguarded parts of the frozen Donetz. Despite the escape of thousands of Red Army troops, German soldiers finally found themselves at almost exactly the same line from where they had first set out the previous winter. The German Army had yet again demonstrated its renowned powers of recovery.

Intoxicated by its success on the Donetz, soldiers recaptured the city of Kharkov, and plans were immediately drawn up for a massive attack on the Kursk salient. Although the German Army had successfully stabilized the Eastern Front, its soldiers had no longer the strength to mount another successful offensive like those seen in 1941 and 1942. Nevertheless, Hitler still tried to once more take the initiative in the East, gambling everything he could muster at Kursk. The German Army was poised in the summer of 1943. Either they gain the initiative, or they were to be driven into a long, painful and bitter retreat.

PART I

Summer 1943–Winter 1943/44

1. Kursk

In July 1943, the German Army launched what proved to be its last great offensive on the Eastern Front – against the Kursk salient. Despite massive losses sustained by their forces at Stalingrad, which led to the subsequent destruction of the 6th Army, Hitler was determined as ever not to give up the fight in Russia. It was here at Kursk that the Führer was confronted with a very tempting strategic opportunity that he was convinced could yield him victory.

Within the huge salient, measuring some 120 miles wide and 75 miles deep, he tried to persuade his generals that his forces could attack from the north and south of the salient in a huge pincer movement and encircle the Red Army. In Hitler's view, the offensive, codenamed 'Zitadelle', would be the greatest armoured battle ever won by both the German Army and Waffen-SS. As with the opening phases of 'Barbarossa' in June 1941, a confident Hitler had predicted that 'he only had to kick in the front door and the whole rotten edifice would come crashing down'.

Despite Hitler's confidence, many of the German generals were not blind to the great difficulties facing them at Kursk. In fact, a number of them were concerned at the enemy's growing strength. Intelligence had already confirmed that the Red Army had constructed a number of major defensive belts, each of which were subdivided into two or even three layers of almost impregnable strongholds. Although there were no real accurate figures, these Soviet belts were some 150 miles deep. Each belt consisted of many anti-tank strong points and an extensive network of obstacles with a maze of intricate blockhouses and trenches. The Russian soldiers that were dug-in along these belts were well camouflaged and heavily armed with plenty of provisions to sustain them during long contact with the enemy.

For three long months the Red Army had been prepared for the German attack. Improved intelligence had allowed Russian commanders to predict exactly the strategic focal point of the German attack. It was this combined collection of battlefield intelligence that proved the ultimate failure of 'Zitadelle', even before it had begun. The German Army were determined to rejuvenate their Blitzkrieg tactics, but the immense preparations that had gone into constructing the Soviet defences meant that the Germans were never ever going to succeed in penetrating into the strategic depths of the Red Army fortifications with any overriding success.

The battle of the Kursk was probably the first modern Soviet operation of the war. Despite the fact that the Red Army lacked the technological superiority of individual weapons, they had a well-prepared defensive programme, which included elaborate deception plans to confuse the enemy.

Order of Battle under German Army Command – 1 July 1943

Army Group Centre
Commander: Field Marshal Gunther von Kluge

2nd Panzer Army
Commander: General Rudolf Schmidt

LV Army Corps

321st Infantry Division
339th Infantry Division
110th Infantry Division
296th Infantry Division
134th Infantry Division

LIII Army Corps

211th Infantry Division
293rd Infantry Division
25th Panzergrenadier-Division
208th Infantry Division
112th Infantry Division [Reserve]

XXXV Army Corps

Commander: General Lothar Rendulic

34th Infantry Division
56th Infantry Division
262nd Infantry Division
299th Infantry Division
36th Infantry Division
5th Panzer Division
8th Panzer Division
305th Security Division
707th Security Division

[Total Strength: 160,000 soldiers, 325 tanks and assault guns]

Ninth Army

Commander: General Walter Model

XXIII Army Corps

Commander: General Johannes Freissner

383rd Infantry Division
216th Infantry Division
78th Assault Division
36th Infantry Division
185th Assault Gun Detachment
189th Assault Gun Detachment

XXXXI Panzer Corps

Commander: General Joseph Harpe

86th Infantry Division
292nd Infantry Division
18th Panzer Division
656th Anti-Tank Detachment
653rd Anti-Tank Detachment
654th Anti-Tank detachment
177th Assault Gun Detachment
244th Assault Gun Detachment
216th Heavy Panzer Detachment
313th Panzer Company
314th Panzer Company
21st Panzer Brigade
909th Assault Gun Detachment
505th Panzer Detachment

XXXXVII Panzer Corps

Commander: General Joachim Lemelsen

6th Infantry Division
2nd Panzer Division
9th Panzer Division
20th Panzer Division
245th Assault Gun Detachment
904th Assault Gun Detachment
312th Panzer Company

XXXXVI Panzer Corps

Commander: General Hans Zorn

31st Infantry Division
7th Infantry Division
258th Infantry Division
102nd Infantry Division

XX Army Corps

Commander: General Freiherr von Roman

72nd Infantry Division
45th Infantry Division
137th Infantry Division
251st Infantry Division

VIII Army Corps

102nd Hungarian Infantry Division
105th Hungarian Infantry Division
108th Hungarian Infantry Division
10th Panzergrenadier Division
12th Panzer Division
4th Panzer Division
203rd Security Division
22nd Security Division

Second Army

Commander: General Walter Weiss

XIII Army Corps

82nd Infantry Division
340th Infantry Division
327th Infantry Division

VII Army Corps

88th Infantry Division
75th Infantry Division
68th Infantry Division
26th Infantry Division
323rd Infantry Division

202nd Anti-Tank Detachment
559th Anti-Tank Detachment
616th Anti-Tank Detachment

[Total Strength: 96,000 men, 925 tanks and 170 assault guns]

Army Group South

Commander: Field Marshal Erich von Manstein

Fourth Panzer Army

Commander: General Hermann Hoth

LII Army Corps

Commander: General Eugen Ott

57th Infantry Division
255th Infantry Division
332nd Infantry Division

XXXXVIII Panzer Corps

Commander: General Otto von Knobelsdorff

3rd Panzer Division
11th Panzer Division
167th Infantry Division
Panzergrenadier Division Grossdeutschland
10th Panzer Brigade
132nd Artillery Command
144th Artillery Command
70th Artillery Regiment
911th Assault Gun Detachment
515th Pioneer Regiment
616th Army Anti-Aircraft Battalion

[Total strength including Waffen-SS troops: 223,907 men, 925 tanks, and 170 assault guns]

Army Detachment Kempf

Commander: General Werner Kempf

XI Army Corps

General Erhard Rauss

106th Infantry Division
320th Infantry Division
52nd Werfer Regiment
4th Anti-Aircraft Regiment
7th Anti-Aircraft Regiment
48th Anti-Aircraft Regiment
18th Pioneer Regiment
153rd Artillery Command
905th Assault Gun Detachment
393rd Assault Gun Company

XXXXII Army Corps

Commander: General Franz Mattenklott

39th Infantry Division
161st Infantry Division
282nd Infantry Division
77th Anti-Aircraft Regiment
560th Heavy Panzer Destroyer
107th Artillery Command

III Panzer Corps

Commander: General Hermann Breith

6th Panzer Division
7th Panzer Division
19th Panzer Division
168th Infantry Division
54th Werfer Regiment
503rd Heavy Panzer Detachment (Tiger)
99th Anti-Aircraft Regiment
153rd Anti-Aircraft Regiment
674th Pioneer Regiment
601st Pioneer Regiment
3rd Artillery Command

[Total Strength: 126,000 men, 344 tanks, and 155 anti-tank and assault guns]

Army Group Centre

During the early morning of 5 July 1943, the long awaited battle began in earnest with the Germans unleashing one of their largest artillery bombardments of the war. In fact, the bombardment was so intense that in no less than one hour the Germans had hurled more shells than they had used in both Poland and the Western Campaign put together. Once the bombardments subsided German ground attacks were ordered forward into action. Their objective was to break through the Kursk-Orel highway and railway and then drive southwards to Kursk.

In order to reduce the vulnerability of the armoured vehicles that were to achieve this ambitious advance, General Walter Model, commander of the 9th Army, insisted that dismounted infantry accompany his armoured vehicles. Although Model's tactics helped reduce tank losses on the first morning, it was at the expense of massive infantry casualties.

During the rest of the first day the 9th Army fell far short of its objectives, due to the fact that the Soviet Central Front had correctly anticipated the attack sector. Attacking on a 25-mile-wide front, the Germans found themselves trapped in the huge defensive minefields, and desperately called upon engineering units to clear them under artillery fire. Although engineering units were able to clear some of the mines, they were generally unsuccessful. As a consequence German losses in the Soviet minefields were massive. The German 653rd Heavy Panzerjäger Battalion, for instance, lost 37 of its 49 Ferdinand self-propelled guns on the first day alone. Although the bulk of these vehicles were regarded as just 'mobility kills', rather than permanent losses, they were nonetheless out of action until they could be repaired.

All over the German northern front troops tried their best to push forward under relentless Russian fire. To the German soldier in this battle, it was unlike any other engagement they had previously encountered. A German grenadier wrote:

> The Red Army soldiers refused to give up. Nor did they panic in the face of our roaring Tiger tanks. The Soviets were cunning in every way. They allowed our tanks to rumble past their well-camouflaged foxholes and then sprang out to deal with the German grenadier following in its wake. Constantly our tanks and assualt guns had to turn back to relive the stranded and often exhausted grenadiers.

In 9th Army, XIII Army Corps was by far the strongest Corps in both in men and anti-tank guns. It faced the strongest defensive positions in the entire salient and was used as a battering ram against the strong Russian defensive positions. But as with all other sectors of the front at Kursk, the Red Army, despite continuing to incur huge losses in both men and weaponry, deprived the XIII Army Corps and the rest of the forces in 9th Army of achieving any of their objectives. The Russians, however, constantly strengthened their defences through reinforcement, skilfully deploying mobile armour and anti-tank reserves to compensate for the high losses.

Within twenty-four hours of the initial attack the 9th Army's 25-mile front had been reduced to some 20 miles. By 7 July this dropped to around 8 miles wide, and the following day only less than a mile. Not only had the front shrank, but the depth of the German attack had been significantly reduced. By 10 July, through sheer weight of Soviet strength and stubborn combat along an ever-extending front, German mobile units of the 9th Army were finally forced to a standstill and were fighting for their lives. Everything that could go wrong for the German 9th Army had been played out on the bloodsoaked plains of Kursk. After a week of the attack the German Army had only moved some 8 miles. On 12 July this prompted the Red Army to launch their offensive against the 2nd Army at Orel. With all their might they began to pulverise the German positions into the ground. The 9th Army were now compelled to withdraw or face total annihilation.

Casualties were huge compared to those sustained by the Russians. Losses in equipment too were substantial. The German Panzer divisions had lost some 300 of their trusted Pz.Kpfw.III & IV's, half a dozen Tiger Is and 50 tank destroyers.

Southern Front

Whilst the Northern Front was continuously hampered by strong enemy resistance, in the south of the salient the Voronezh Front fared less well against the German Army and its elite SS counterparts of the II SS Panzer Corps. These units of Army Group South were very powerful and consisted of an immense phalanx of armour. One of the most powerful armoured forces consisted of Hoth's 4th.Panzer Army. This armoured force had achieved remarkable progress on the first day of the attack and had successfully spearheaded its way forward forcing its way through strong Russian defences. By 6 July it had smashed its way through Red Army lines and radioed that the advanced elements were some 9 miles beyond their start lines.

Along the rest of the southern front other German forces were making equally good progress against the Red Army. But as in the north, attack frontages and penetration depth were reduced as the attack proceeded. Consequently within three days the front had been reduced from a 16 mile front to 1½ miles. Yet again the Russians had heroically held their positions to the last man. The many thousands of mines and artillery pieces were again successful in delaying the German attack and inflicting appalling losses on the Germans. In fact, across threatened sectors of the front where German forces seemed to penetrate areas more deeply the Russians quickly brought up additional stocks of mines. Over 90,000 of these mines alone were laid during the battle by small mobile groups of engineers at night. Once again the Germans fell victim to the mines. Within five days of heavy fighting many German units had lost immeasurable amounts of men and equipment. The elite Großdeutschland Division for instance, which began the battle with 118 tanks, only had 3 Tigers, 6 Panthers, and 11 Pz.Kpfw.III's and IV tanks left operational. The XLVIII Panzer Corps reported, overall, 38 Panthers operational with 131 awaiting repair, out of the 200 it started with on 5 July.

By 12 July the Red Army had finally ground down the German Army at Kursk and threw its offensive timetable off schedule. For the first time in the war the Soviets had savagely contested every foot of ground and were finally on an equal footing. The German offensive at Kursk had dealt them a severe battering from which they were never to properly recover. They had lost some 30 divisions, including seven Panzer divisions. According to official Soviet sources, as many as 49,822 German troops were killed or missing. They had lost a staggering 1,614 tanks and self-propelled guns that were committed to action. As for the Red Army, they suffered much higher losses with some 177,847 being killed and injured. They lost 2,586 Soviet tanks and self-propelled guns during the operation. The battle of Kursk had finally ended the myth of German invincibility and was the first time that the blitzkrieg concept had failed. As for the German Army the tide had finally turned. They lost the initiative in the East and now had begun a fighting withdrawal.

PART I: SUMMER 1943–WINTER 1943/44

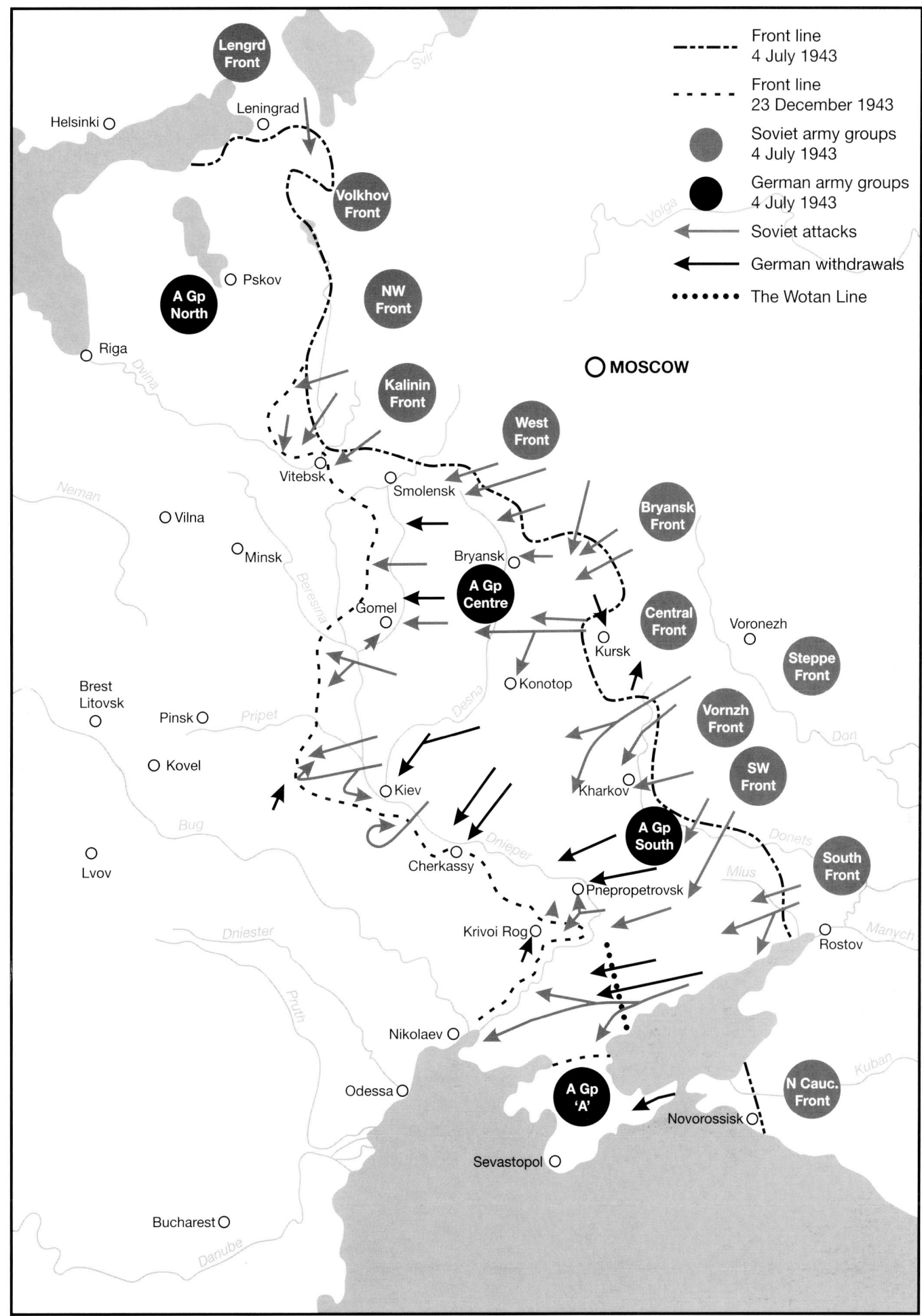

Map 1: Eastern Front, Kursk and subsequent Soviet counter-offensives and offensives, July–December 1943

German troops move forward into action during the early stage of 'Operation Zitadelle' in July 1943. In front of the German Army at Kursk stood six major defensive belts, each of which were subdivided into two or even three layers of almost impregnable strongholds. The first two belts were occupied by troops, while units that were held in reserve occupied the third and fourth belts. (HITM)

A machine gun crew with their MG34 machine gun fitted to a *Dreifuss* fire mount tripod directs their gun skyward after detecting an enemy aircraft in the area. The primary gunner was known as the Schütze 1, whilst his teammate, Schütze 2, fed the ammunition belts and saw that the gun remained operational. The other men in the crew brought up fresh ammunition for the gun. (HITM)

PART I: SUMMER 1943–WINTER 1943/44

Luftwaffe field division troops preparing to use a Pak gun against a Russian target during operations at Kursk in July 1943. On the Eastern Front the Luftwaffe field divisions were simply thrown into combat without proper training or leadership. Even by the time that some units saw action at Kursk there were still serious doubts as to the combat effectiveness of the Luftwaffe fighting alongside the German Army. However, by November 1943 the army finally took full command of these formations. (HITM)

A soldier peers through scissor binoculars, which have been covered with foliage to help conceal them in the long tall grass of the Kursk plains in the summer of 1943. The scissor binoculars were commonly known as 'donkey ears', for obvious reasons. The two lenses were designed especially to be further apart than a pair of human eyes and were able to determine ranges much more successfully. (HITM)

A halftrack negotiates some uneven terrain as it moves forward into action towing a 15cm artillery piece during the early stages of 'Zitadelle'. The artillery bombardment that opened up the German offensive at Kursk was massive. After it subsided infantry and armour poured forward with artillery units following in the wake of the forward spearheads. (HITM)

An MG34 machine gun team pass through a destroyed Russian town. Even during the Kursk offensive German MG34 machine gunners were able to hold up attacking infantry many times their number. In fact, just a couple of well-sited, camouflaged and adequately-supplied machine guns could hold up an entire attacking unit on a frontage of at least 5 miles or more. (HITM)

PART I: SUMMER 1943–WINTER 1943/44

A 7.5cm Panzerjäger Marder III moves along a dusty road during the Kursk offensive in July 1943. On the Eastern Front the Marder III quickly proved its tactical worth, as it was more than capable of destroying a T-34 tank at normal combat ranges. German troops found the Marder a useful weapon for mobile armoured support and as a result managed to advance deeper into enemy territory. (HITM)

Here a Pz.Kpfw VI Tiger I has halted on a dirt track inside a forest clearing during the summer of 1943. At Kursk the Tiger I played a crucial part in the offensive and demonstrated its awesome killing power. Although the Tiger was used extensively by the Waffen-SS at Kursk the German Army too used the Tiger. Walther Model had two companies of 14 Tigers each, whilst in the south von Manstein's Army Group South had a separate unit of 45 Tigers, plus one Tiger company in the Grossdeutschland Division. (HITM)

A Panzerjäger Tiger (P) Elefant Tank Destroyer being prepared to be transported on board a railway flatcar. Armed with a powerful Pak 43/2 L/71 8.8cm flak gun this beast was capable of defeating all types of Soviet tanks, but it lacked cross-country mobility and was prone to breakdowns. (HITM)

During the early stages of the Kursk offensive a halftrack moves along a road pulling a 15cm artillery piece. The halftrack was used extensively by the German Army throughout the war. It was regarded as a unique way of not only towing various guns to the forward edge of the battlefield, but the crew as well. (HITM)

PART I: SUMMER 1943–WINTER 1943/44

A Wespe self-propelled artillery gun belonging to the armoured artillery regiment of the Grossdeutschland division negotiates some rough terrain south of Obojan during the Kursk offensive in July 1943. (HITM)

A close-up view of an MG34 machine gunner using the optical sight provided with heavy machine-guns. The machine gunner holds the rank of an Obergefreiter or corporal and is wearing the standard regulation German Army issue camouflage helmet cover. (HITM)

A halftrack crosses a pontoon bridge in the summer of 1943. By this period of the war the German Army were fighting for survival. Everything would now hinge on the successful outcome of the Kursk offensive. Failure would undoubtedly result in a long painful and costly retreat. (HITM)

A Pz.Kpfw VI Tiger I has been loaded onto a special railway flatcar destined to join the frontline during operations on the Eastern Front in the summer of 1943. It was vital for both the German Army and the Waffen-SS to transport vital armour as quickly as possible in order to help support front lines and prevent them from collapse. (HITM)

PART I: SUMMER 1943–WINTER 1943/44

New PzKpfw V Panther tanks at a field maintenance workshop on the Eastern Front during the summer of 1943. These medium tanks, which were developed as a direct response to the Russian T-34, saw their debut at Kursk. During the first twelve days of fighting the Panther strength was reduced to only 10 tanks; 123 were lost or damaged by enemy fire whilst the remaining 46 developed mechanical failures. (HITM)

The crew of an eight-wheeled radio vehicle has halted in a field during the Kursk offensive in July 1943. The vehicle was equipped with a long-range radio set and was used mainly by signal units and Army headquarters. Foliage has been attached to parts of the vehicle in order to help conceal it from aerial attack. (HITM)

FROM RETREAT TO DEFEAT

A halftrack pulling an artillery piece halts at a river before resuming its advance in the Kursk region in the summer of 1943. Operation 'Zitadelle' was not as ambitious as previous offensives in the East. However, Hitler thought a victory in the Kursk salient would restore his army's morale especially after the disaster at Stalingrad. (HITM)

Pioneers have halted with their vehicle during operations in the Kursk salient. This photograph was taken near Belgorod where the 6th Panzer Division unleashed its mighty force on 5 July and attacked strong Red Army defences. (HITM)

A halftrack armed with a 3.7cm flak gun moves through a Russian village during the summer of 1943. On board the halftrack space for the crew was at a premium. In action the sides of the gun platform could be folded down in order to provide additional space for the crew to manoeuvre around the gun. Note the halftrack towing a single axial trailer with additional ammunition. (HITM)

The crew of PzKpfw III rest onboard their vehicle during the summer campaign of 1943. Behind them is another halted PzKpfw III. During the early stages of the war in the East the PzKpfw III had shown its worth on the battlefield, but as they were confronted with ever increasing amounts of T-34s and KV-1 heavy tanks it was soon recognized as an inadequate weapon. By the time Kursk arrived, they were obsolete. This battle proved to be the last great armoured encounter in which the PzKpfw III was involved in large numbers. (HITM)

A halftrack with a full compliment of crew advances along a dusty road towing a 15cm artillery piece during the Kursk offensive. (HITM)

A column of Tiger tanks with infantry onboard move along a dusty road during the summer of 1943. At Kursk the Tiger was the most lethal tank on the battlefield. It could decimate Soviet tank formations from ranges over 1,000 metres, where it was invulnerable to Russian return fire. (HITM)

PART I: SUMMER 1943–WINTER 1943/44

As the greatest tank battle unfolded at Kursk the 5th Gebirgsjäger Division had been transferred to Army Group South. Here in this photograph on a relatively quite sector of the front a MG34 machine crew can be seen with their weapon on a *dreifuss* or tripod mounting. After the failure at Kursk these mountain troopers would be embroiled in heavy combat as the Red Army poured westward through to the Crimea. (HITM)

A Pz.Kpfw.IV Ausf.G moves across a field in preparation for the Kursk offensive. This Panzer belongs to the 4th Panzer Division. Average losses to the division during the battle were around three-quarters of its original strength. What was left of the decimated division withdrew westward towards the Dniepr and Pripyet rivers where it began a series of aggressive defensive operations which carried on into December 1943. (HITM)

A MG34 machine gunner in a defensive position during the Kursk offensive. The machine gun has been attached to a MG *Lafette 34* sustained-fire mount. The gunner uses a grip trigger that has a mechanical linkage to the trigger on the gun. (HITM)

A column of halftracks has halted on a dusty road during the summer of 1943. In spite of a very impressive force the missions assigned to the German Army in the East that summer were immense, especially after the great losses suffered during the winter. The setting of objectives was now of key importance for the outcome of the entire war in the East. (HITM)

A MG34 machine gunner with ammunition feeder during the Kursk offensive. The MG34 machine gun was one of the most popular weapons used by the German Army during the war. It had tremendous defensive staying power against enemy infantry and during the last two years of the war soldiers took to continuously deploying their machine guns in the most advantageous defensive positions. (HITM)

A halftrack towing an 8.8cm flak gun crosses what appears to be a damaged wooden bridge. The weight of the vehicle has obviously caused the bridge to collapse into the river, making crossing more hazardous. (HITM)

During the summer of 1943 a MG34 machine gunner can be seen with his gun slung over his left shoulder for ease of carriage. The MG34 weighed 11.5kg (25.4lb), possessed a wooden shoulder stock, a pistol grip and a V-notch rear sight. (HITM)

Soldiers of the 5th Gebirgsjäger Division during operations in southern Russia in the late summer of 1943. A MG34 machine gunner can be seen with the weapon attached to a tripod. Note the *Edelweiss* insignia on the soldiers' field caps. After the German defeat at Kursk the Red Army launched a massive offensive along a 400-mile front in the south. Over 2,500,000 Red Army troops were thrown at a German Army only half as strong. (HITM)

PART I: SUMMER 1943–WINTER 1943/44

2. Fighting Withdrawal

Following the catastrophe at Kursk German warfare was now on the defensive. But in spite of the German failure at Kursk, the German High Command still clung to the view that fighting there had squeezed all available resources out of the Red Army. They ardently believed that the rest of the summer campaign could be devoted to a series of tactical solutions that could straighten out the front and prepare its defences for the onset of the winter. The German soldier now believed that he belonged to the weaker army and had to accept that offensive and defensive operations had to be altered with the seasons. To the soldier this undoubtedly prolonged the agony of fighting on the Eastern Front. Indeed, throughout the whole summer of 1943 the German Army had suffered permanent change. It had lost its courage and the will to advance. Hope was tainted by the growing prospect of being sucked into another bloody protracted battle and being cut-off and literally annihilated by its giant foe. With nothing but a string of defeats in its wake the German Army reluctantly withdrew across Russia.

In southern Russia a number of advanced units of Army Group South tried their best to hold onto vital areas of ground in order to contain the overly-extended front. By the end of July 1943 Army Group South had a total of 822,000 troops opposing an estimated 1,710,000 Russians. The army group had 1,161 tanks, about half of them operational, whilst the Russians had 2,872 tanks. Here in the south the majority of units were seriously understrength and still further depleted by vehicles constantly being taken out for repair. This undoubtedly left a substantial lack of armour to support the troops on the front lines. Consequently Army Group South was finally forced to withdraw and avoid being cut off through deep enemy breakthroughs and suffer the same fait as that of the 6th Army at Stalingrad. At the end of July a substantial amount of men and equipment had withdrawn into the Donetz area.

Further north in the middle sector of the Eastern Front Army Group Centre were trying desperately to hold the Red Army from breaking through their lines. But their strength too had been severely weakened by the battle of Kursk. By 5 August the Russians captured Orel. Simultaneous drives along the southern sector of the front saw the Red Army take Kharkov, the most fought-over city in Russia. Soviet troops then pressed forward and crossed the Donetz. These powerful drives soon threatened to envelop General Kleist's Army Group A, which was still bitterly contesting every foot of ground in the Crimea. It seemed that large parts of the German southern front would soon be overrun, but on 31 August Hitler reluctantly ordered further withdrawals. The Hitler 'Order' averted a catastrophe, but it only temporarily stabilised the front. Already Army Group Centre had been pierced in three places and the whole sector in that part of the Eastern Front begun to disintegrate under the sheer weight of the Red Army. By 8 September advanced Russian units were reported to be no less than 30 miles from the Dnieper and by 14 September were threatening the city of Kiev. On 15 September Hitler once again ordered another withdrawal, this time his forces were to be moved back to the line of the Dnieper, Sozh and Pronya rivers, approximately the line reached by the German Army during their victorious 'Barbarossa' campaign in July 1941. However, the instruction to permit an ordered withdrawal came too late. What followed was thousands of German soldiers frantically racing for the river positions with Red Army troops smashing onto a number of formations and totally annihilating them. By 30 September the Russians had five bridgeheads over the Dnieper.

For the German Army on the Eastern Front the summer campaign of 1943 had been completely disastrous. During five weeks of almost continuous bloody fighting it had withdrawn some 150-miles along a 650-mile front. Whilst these forces retreated Hitler had decreed a 'Scorched Earth Policy', in which the main roads, railway lines, power stations, farms and factories were to be destroyed. However, in all the panic and confusion, the demolition teams did not have enough time to implement the destruction of the main roads along which the Red Army used for its main advance.

As the winter of 1943/44 reared its head during October, a feeling of further despair and gloom prevailed across the German Army. To the depressed soldiers that had to endure the third Russian winter a dull conviction quickly gripped them that the war in the East was lost – yet without any sight of its end. The German Army was still dug deep into the heartlands of Soviet Russia. But unlike 1941 and 1942, they had lost the initiative. Slowly and defiantly the German soldier retreated across a bleak and hostile landscape, always outnumbered, constantly low on fuel, ammunition and other desperate supplies. In three months following the defeat at Kursk Army Group South alone had only received some 32,000 replacements, although it suffered more than 130,000 casualties. The equipment situation too continued to decline, especially in Panzer units. The whole of the German Army in the East was thus faced with a dangerous and worsening prospect than ever before. To make matters worse, an anti-partisan conflict added yet another dimension to the war in Russia. With word of the advancing Red Army, Ukrainian nationalist partisans, Polish underground groups and communist partisans began raiding German outposts, barracks, police stations, rail depots, supply dumps, ambushing convoys and trains. As the

German troops withdrew they had to clear out the partisans before they became prey to the snipers and saboteurs. All this, and continuous pressure from Hitler to defend every yard of land with their blood, made fighting even more inhumane. For the German Army the closing months of 1943 passed, like the autumn, in a sequence of bitter bloodthirsty battles, which consequently sapped the will and energy of German strength almost beyond repair.

PART I: SUMMER 1943–WINTER 1943/44

On the retreat, German troops march to a new position following the failure of Operation Zitadelle. Kursk had finally marked the turning point in the war for the German Army strategically, operationally, and tactically. (HITM)

Here a MG34 machine gun team fight for survival following the disaster at Kursk. The battles that followed Operation Zitadelle not only ended the myth of German invincibility in the East but also clearly demonstrated that the Red Army was rapidly developing into a skilful army with enormous quantities of men and material. (HITM)

One of the quickest and effective forms of transporting armour on the Eastern Front from one battlefront to another was by rail. Here halftracks with artillery together with support vehicles are seen preparing to be moved, late 1943. (HITM)

A whitewashed PzKpfw IV during operations in southern Russia in November 1943. After the German defeat at Kursk, Army Group South tried its best to hold onto vital areas of ground in order to contain the overly extended front. (HITM)

PART I: SUMMER 1943–WINTER 1943/44

Panzergrenadiers withdraw across a bleak and devastated landscape. For weeks the German Army was compelled yet again to fight in the mud and freezing weather with no end to the war. In spite of the mounting casualties Hitler still prohibited all voluntary withdrawals. (HITM)

Panzer crews debate their next move during operations in late October 1943. After the defeat of the German Army at Kursk the *Panzerwaffe* was a shadow of its former self. Each Panzer division now averaged 98 tanks and self-propelled guns, not including self-propelled anti-tank guns. Every division in the East was so weak that it could not contain the enemy for any appreciable length of time. (HITM)

Halftracks towing artillery in the late winter of 1943. Losses suffered in the continuous battles of 1943 and the beginning of 1944 would further weaken and reduce the effectiveness of the German Army. Time was now running out. (HITM)

On the German Northern Front a 15cm artillery gun is being prepared for action during the winter of 1943. In the north the German Army, notably the 16th and 18th Armies, were already badly depleted and were required to hold back far superior Russian forces. (HITM)

PART I: SUMMER 1943–WINTER 1943/44

This marvellously clear study shows heavily-laden German infantry during a short pause, the southern sector of the Eastern Front, early 1944. (Ullstein Bilderdienst)

Soldiers pose for the camera in the snow in front of a whitewashed PzKpfw III. Most of the men are wearing reversible winter clothing. Apart from being extremely comfortable and warm, these uniforms provided the wearer with greater freedom of movement, especially with personal equipment. (HITM)

A halftrack towing a 8.8cm flak gun is seen moving through a frozen river. This photograph was taken in late December 1943 close to the Luga River. By this period of the war the entire German Northern Front was on the point of disintegration. Within weeks the Russians had unleashed a massive offensive that would see the city of Leningrad liberated. (HITM)

PART I: SUMMER 1943–WINTER 1943/44

Soldiers from Army Group South observe enemy positions through a pair of scissors binoculars, January 1944. Note the Soviet PPsH submachine gun in the foreground - this reliable weapon was very popular with German soldiers until the end of the war. (Ullstein Bilderdienst)

Fighting in extreme arctic conditions during late 1943 early 1944. One soldier can be seen armed with a MG34 machine gun, whilst his comrades are holding standard bolt-action rifles. The Kar98 carbine bolt-action rifle was the standard issue piece of weaponry supplied to the German Army throughout the war. (HITM)

A Panzer crew confers with the aid of maps and debates its next move on the battlefield. Between 1 September and 31 December 1943, German armoured forces on the Eastern Front averaged 2,000 tanks, of which only 800 were combat ready at any one time. (HITM)

Two MG34 machine gunners and crew scour the terrain trying to deduce the location of advancing Soviet forces during the winter of 1943. By this period of the war in the East, German infantry divisions had been severely mauled. A number had suffered serious losses, but could be re-equipped without withdrawing them completely from combat. In many cases, the high losses resulted from inadequate supplies and the insufficient skill and determination of many of the allied armies that had joined the war against Russia. (HITM)

PART II

Winter 1943/44–Autumn 1944

3. Winter warfare

The military situation on the Eastern Front in January 1944 was dire for the German Army. It had entered into the New Year with a dwindling number of soldiers to man the battle lines. The Red Army, however, was now in even greater strength than ever before and Hitler's reluctance to concede territory was still proving to be very problematic for commanders in the field. The persistent lack of strategic direction in the East was causing major trouble too. Nevertheless, in spite of the worsening condition of the German Army, the soldiers were compelled to fight on.

In Army Group North, General George von Kuechler's force had been for some weeks trying in vain to hold its positions along its northern defences against strong Russian forces. From the Volkhov River to the Gulf of Finland the front was covered with a string of trenches and shell holes, reminiscent of trench warfare during World War One. By 15 January 1944, the defences were finally attacked by three Soviet fronts, the Leningrad, Volkhov and Second Baltic. The 18th Army, which bore the brunt of the main attacks, were outnumbered by at least 3:1 in divisions. As usual the German troops were expected to hold the front, but the overwhelming enemy firepower proved too much and Kuechler's Army Group was compelled to fall back under a hurricane of enemy fire. Within four days of the attack the Russians had successfully breached Army Group North's defences in three places. This effectively wrenched open a huge corridor allowing Red Army troops to pour through towards the besieged city of Leningrad. Troops of the German 18th Army were beginning to disintegrate. Already it had incurred 40,000 casualties trying to contain the Soviets. Fighting in the mud and freezing water, the men were totally exhausted and unable to hold back the enemy for any appreciable length of time. Hitler on the other hand still prohibited all voluntary withdrawals and reserved all decisions to withdraw to himself. In a leadership conference held by the Führer the commanders were told to infuse determination in their men and to strengthen faith in ultimate victory. But in spite of Hitler's radical measures in trying to generate the will to fight until success was secured, the German Army were unable to stem the rout of the advancing Russian forces.

By 26 January the city of Leningrad was liberated after nine hundred days of siege. The 18th Army was now split into three parts and struggled to hold any type of front forward of the Luga River. The entire German Northern Front was now beginning to crumble and Hitler openly blamed Kuechler for its failure. On 1 February 1944 the General was relived of his command and temporarily replaced by Hitler's Eastern Front 'trouble shooter', General Walther Model. Model was a great improviser who was quite capable of changing the tactical situation in Army Group North. Almost immediately Model went to work by introducing his '*Schild und Schwert*' (Shield and Sword) policy, which stated that no soldiers were to withdraw without his express permission, only if they paved the way for a counterstroke later. Along the front both the 16th and 18th Armies, which were badly depleted with only the 12th Panzer and 58th Infantry divisions, intact were ordered to hold the line on the Luga River, east of a series of heavily constructed defences known as the Panther Line. Model, determined at all costs to prevent the front degenerating into a panic flight collected stragglers and sent them back to the line. He cancelled leaves, sent walking wounded to their units, and sent a number of the rear-echelon troops to the front. Without hesitation he requested more reinforcements, which included Waffen-SS replacements, naval coastal batteries and Luftwaffe troops.

Throughout February morale was temporarily restored to the frontline units and as the German forces stepped back to defend the Panther Line they had slightly gained enough strength to hold back the Red Army. During March the Russians began exerting more pressure, especially against the 16th Army that was defending positions along the Baltic. But the spring thaw had arrived early and melting snow had turned the roads on which the Russians were travelling into a quagmire. The conditions were so bad that forward units from the 16th Army reported that Soviet tanks could be seen sinking up to their turrets in mud. It seemed the Panther Line was holding, with the weather playing a major part in containing the Red Army. Now it would not be until the early summer that the Red Army would resume its push. Thanks to Model, Army Group North was now stabilised. Due to his energetic, innovative and courageous method of leadership he had prevented the wholesale collapse of the northern sector of the Eastern Front.

Model's success in the north now earned him a new command in Army Group South. On 30 March 1944, less than a week before Army Group South was redesignated Army Group North Ukraine, Model replaced Manstein and was installed as Commander-in-Chief.

For three long months Army Group South had fought a series of bitter and bloody battles in order to stem the gradual deterioration of its forces in southern Russia. Conditions for the German Army between January and March 1944 were dismal. Supplies were inadequate, and replacements in men were far below what was needed to sustain its divisions along the entire front. To make matters worse in early January a 110-mile breach between Army Group Centre and Army Group South had developed. Neither army group had sufficient forces to plug the gap and by the end of the month the gap opened even wider when the Belorussian Front pushed the 2nd Army to the line of the Ipa River.

For the next few weeks' further pressure was applied on Army Group South. By this time the German front was disintegrating under persistent overwhelming enemy attacks. German mobile reserves had all been worn down to almost extinction and this led to a number of units being encircled. One of the largest pockets to develop was in the Kovel-Korsun area of the lower Dnieper where seven German divisions and the 5th SS Wiking Division were trapped. By using some of the last Panzers in the area, Manstein managed to drive a wedge and create a corridor for the encircled men and held it open to allow them to escape. The remnants of the shattered divisions that successfully broke out struggled southeast under continuous Russian fire.

To the north of Kovel-Korsun the situation for the rest of Manstein's Army Group was equally dire. The bulk of the men were totally exhausted. The worn out 1st and 4th Panzer armies were all that were left to support troop operations in the south, and they were being slowly compressed against the Carpathian Mountains. By early March advanced Soviet units had reached the outskirts of the city of Tarnopol. Within days of their arrival Red Army troops advanced through the ravaged city but were soon beaten back by strong German defences. As German soldiers fought for Tarnopol Hitler issued another Führer Order appealing for his forces on the Eastern Front to use towns, cities and surrounding areas as fortified positions in order to slow the Soviet drive westward. In other words he was calling upon every soldier to hold to the last man. Many soldiers that were given this awesome task of defending the towns and cites nicknamed these suicidal assignments as *Himmelfahrts-Kommandos* ('missions to Heaven'). In total, Hitler designated some twenty-six cities and larger towns on still occupied Soviet territory as fortified positions; among those in the south were Tarnopol, Proskurov, Kovel, Brody, Vinnitsa, and Pervomaysk.

In the city of Tarnopol conditions for the troops were appalling. For days they held out inside the ruins whilst being subjected to a number of sustained bombardments from heavy Soviet artillery. By 21 March, the Red Army had amassed enough strength to smash the front between Tarnopol and Proskurov. With one single blow 200 tanks of the 1st and 4th Tank Armies smashed through the front swiftly carrying along with them like driftwood, remnants of the German defensive line consisting mainly of the 68th Infantry and 7th Panzer Divisions. Two days later the Russian 1st Tank Army force wheeled west with all its might and hammered its way through bewildered German infantry divisions that were defending Tarnopol. Those troops that were defending surrounding areas were thrown back some ten miles, leaving behind a garrison inside the doomed city. Some of the defenders of Tarnopol reported that the scenes were reminiscent of Stalingrad. For the next three weeks the four thousand strong garrison held out. When a rescue operation by the 9th SS Panzer Division tried to relieve the trapped force only fifty-three men managed to break out during the night of April 15/16 and reach the German lines. The rest were captured or killed.

In spite of the horrifying casualties and huge losses of equipment inflicted upon Army Group South, its forces as a whole during the winter of 1944 had generally defended its positions relatively well against terrible odds. In fact in some places it even held the line. When Model replaced Manstein at the end of March the crises in the south was temporarily relieved as the Russian winter offensive gradually died away. The Red Army after nearly eight months of continuous forward movement had a last given the German Army respite. However, unbeknown to Army Group South, the Russians were preparing for a massive attack against the German centre, which was to carry them to the banks of the river Vistula in Poland. The German Army was soon to be vanquished forever from the Soviet Union.

FROM RETREAT TO DEFEAT

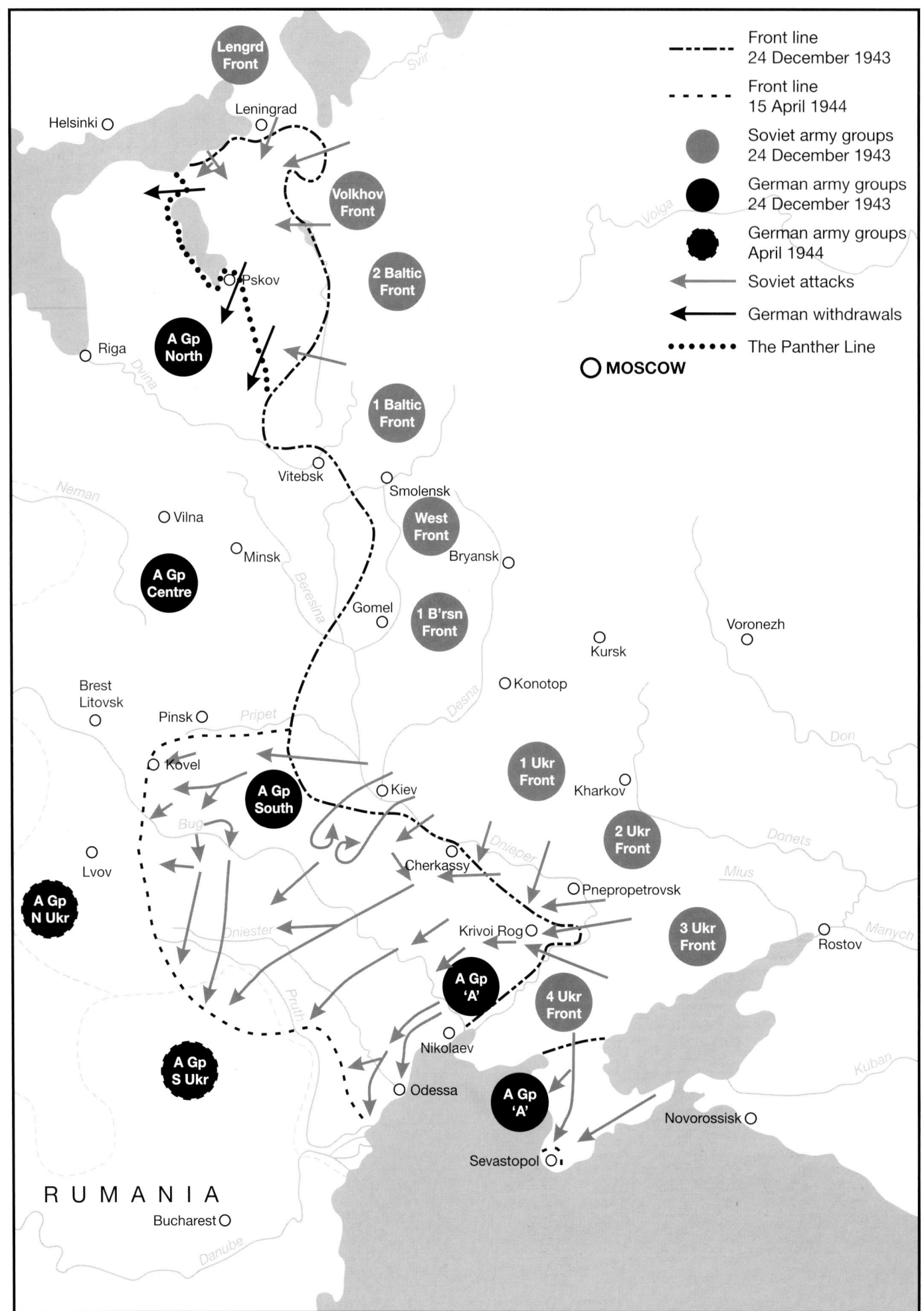

Map 2: Eastern Front, further German withdrawals December 1943-May 1944

PART II: WINTER 1943/44–AUTUMN 1944

A German MG34 crew wearing white camouflage smocks advance through a forest during intensive fighting with Red Army forces near Leningrad in January 1944. By 26 January the city of Leningrad was finally liberated. (HITM)

German troops withdraw westward following the capture of Leningrad. The men are wearing the two-piece snowsuit and their steel helmets have received an application of whitewash for camouflage. Life in the line for these soldiers was a continuous grind. There was little respite – if the Red Army let up for a brief period, the sub zero temperatures certainly did not. (HITM)

A halftrack moves across the frozen plains of northern Russia during the 18th Army's withdrawal from the Leningrad sector of operations in January 1944. With the capture of the city, the 18th Army was split into three parts and desperately struggled to hold any type of front. (HITM)

In February 1944 both the German 16th and 18th Armies were ordered to hold the line on the Luga River, east of a series of heavily constructed defences known as the Panther Line. Here two German troops sit in one of the many miles of well-dug trenches where they were ordered to hold their positions at all costs. (HITM)

PART II: WINTER 1943/44–AUTUMN 1944

German troops take cover by lying in the snow during defensive actions in Army Group North's sector in February 1944. During this period the German Army had actually managed to temporarily strengthen its defences in the region and hold back the Red Army. However, conditions for the men were appalling. (HITM)

Two soldiers wearing white camouflage smocks pose for the camera inside a trench along the Panther Line in early February 1944. Although the white camouflage smocks were a popular item of winter clothing soldiers tended to wear them day and night for weeks on end. Soon they became filthy, thus defeating the objective of the white camouflage. (HITM)

47

At a maintenance depot in 1944 two crewmembers can be seen with a late variant StuG III. By 1944 the StuG III had become a very popular assault gun on the battlefield. The vehicles had initially provided crucial mobile fire support to the infantry, and also proved their worth as an invaluable anti-tank weapon. However, during 1944 as the Eastern Front receded further west the StuG was primarily used as an anti-tank weapon, thus depriving the infantry of vital fire support. (HITM)

A Marder II Panzerjäger advances across a frozen field in early 1944. The Marder series was built in direct response to the heavier Russian tanks and they were used as mobile anti-tank weapons. They proved very popular vehicles on the Eastern Front and were seen on the battlefield until the end of the war. (HITM)

PART II: WINTER 1943/44–AUTUMN 1944

Three soldiers sit on a sled during the harsh winter of early 1944. The men are obviously using this mode of transport as the easiest and quickest method of moving across the snow. Frequently soldiers found advancing through snow on foot was particularly difficult in many areas and quite exhausting. Many modes of transport were used as transportation, but the horse and sledge was normally the most convenient. (HITM)

A StuG III with its crew during the winter of 1944. With its low silhouette for better survivability, the StuG III not only gave sterling service when on the offensive, but also fought brilliantly during defensive battles as well. During 1944 the StuG III played a crucial part in defending a number areas of the front from disintegration. (HITM)

FROM RETREAT TO DEFEAT

Gebirgsjäger troops build an igloo during defensive operations in Army Group North. The building of igloos was most effective in the extreme cold of the Northern Front, but this type of shelter was initially unpopular with German forces. Even so, the igloo was often the only chance to create adequate shelter when all forms of cover were unavailable. (HITM)

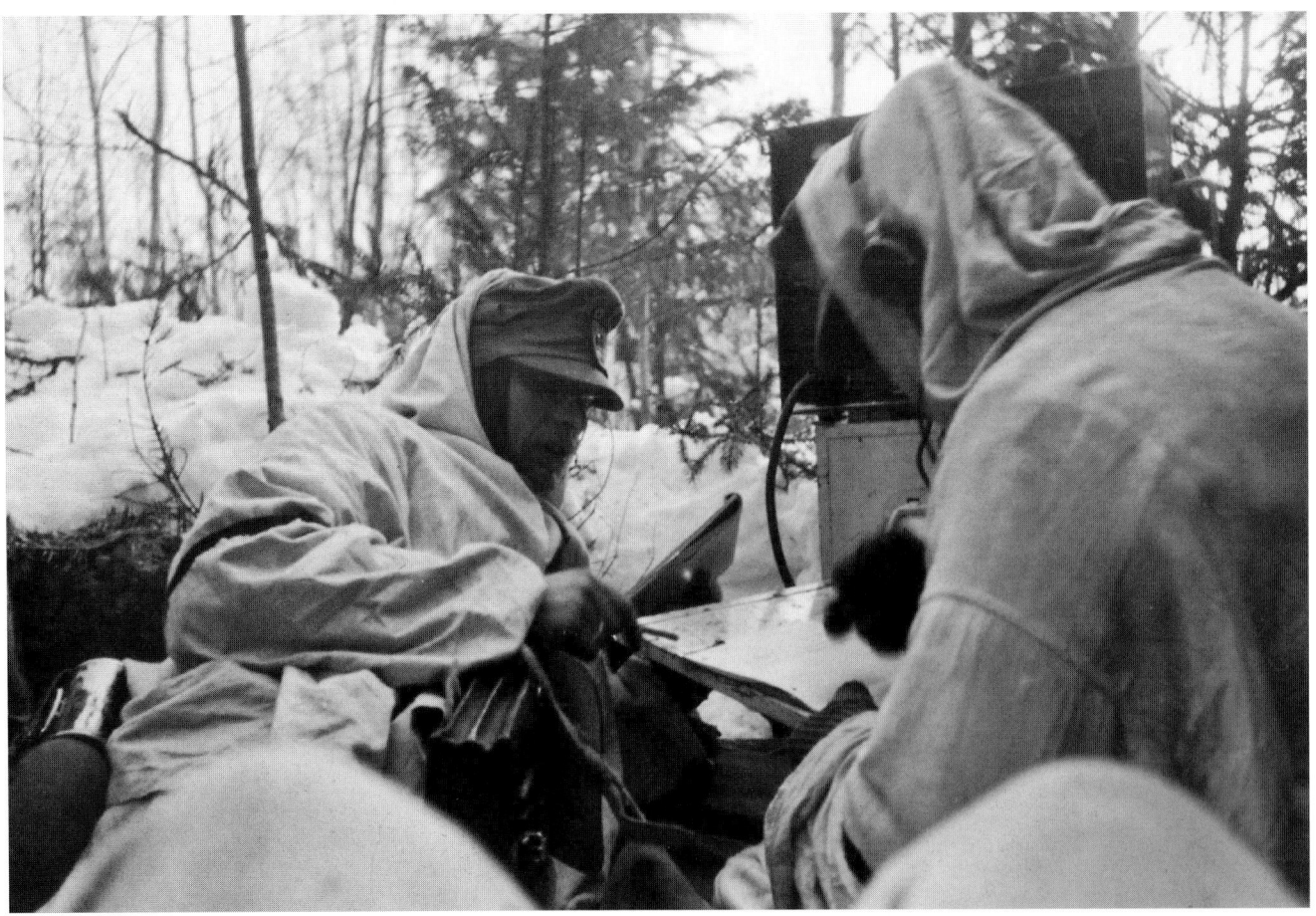

Gebirgsjäger signal operators during operations in the early winter of 1944. These men are more than likely to be a forward observation post, from where they can send through details of enemy movements back to divisional headquarters. (HITM)

PART II: WINTER 1943/44–AUTUMN 1944

A German soldier jokes with local Russian women during the 16th Army's withdrawal to the Panther Line in early 1944. The local inhabitants regularly worked for the German Army and undertook various tasks, which varied considerably from collecting wood and food, to digging immense anti-tank trenches. (HITM)

A column of PzKpfw IVs from Army Group South advancing across the vast Soviet plains. The tanks have all received a coating of winter whitewash paint. Despite inferior numbers the PzKpfw IV fought extremely well in western Russia and scored successes in a number of defensive actions. (HITM)

A 2cm self-propelled flak gun mounted on the back of a halftrack tractor seen here in Army Group South during early 1944. By this period of the war losses had been very high, with many extremely effective units being virtually annihilated. Although the average German soldier proved capable of meeting the highest standards, fighting courageously with self-sacrifice against massive numerical superiority, he could only delay the enemy, not defeat him. (HITM)

A Volkswagen Kubelwagen is parked in the snow during operations in early 1944. The Kubelwagen was originally designed as a civilian vehicle, but was soon adapted for military use. The type 82 was used for reconnaissance and communication purposes. (HITM)

PART II: WINTER 1943/44–AUTUMN 1944

A MG34 machine gun crew during the battle in the Cherkassy pocket in January 1944. In side the pocket some 60,000 German troops had been encircled. Constant pressure was maintained on the encirclement, and although there were frantic appeals by German commanders to be allowed to retreat, Hitler would not listen, insisting his forces remain in place. (HITM)

Two greatcoat clad troops ride on a sled pulled by pony in the vast wastelands of Russia in 1944. Throughout the winter periods in the East the German Army relied heavily on these sleds and ponies for moving supplies and equipment. With the severe lack of motorized transport they were a vital form of transportation. (HITM)

A Volkswagen Kubelwagen Type 82 halted in the snow. The Kubelwagen Type 82 featured a very reliable 4-cylinder, horizontally opposed, air-cooled engine, capable of 23.5hp at 3000rpm and providing a top speed of 80km/h. These were very popular vehicles with over 50,000 Kubelwagens produced by the end of the war. (HITM)

Two heavy MG34 machine gunners are seen here departing from the entrance of their dugout. This photograph was taken on the Panther Line in February 1944, during which time the front lines had been temporarily restored. Within a month the Red Army were once again threatening large areas of the line. (HITM)

PART II: WINTER 1943/44–AUTUMN 1944

Winter of 1944 and a group of Gebirgsjäger troops can be seen wearing their distinctive white camouflage smocks. The mountain troopers were expert in alpine warfare, but it was the ability to operate on skis in severe cold that was of most value. (HITM)

A MG34 machine gunner belonging to the Gebirgsjäger. The soldier has taken off his skis and sits in a shell hole, which affords some protection from the vast open plains of southern Russia. Each Gebirgsjäger soldier had to learn the survival techniques necessary to enable him to survive in the harshest of conditions. He was trained to build primitive shields of rocks around him and utilise the surrounding terrain to protect him against the cold and enemy. (HITM)

Gebirgsjäger officers confer. The headgear worn by all mountain troops of the German Army was the standard headgear issued to all branches of the service and this included those at officer level. This one-piece headgear specific to the Gebirgsjäger was called the *Bergmütze* or mountain cap. (HITM)

A MG34 machine gun on *Dreifuss* fire mount, with the gunner scouring the sky looking for enemy aircraft. (HITM)

Gebirgsjäger transport troops with their pack mules during an blizzard on the Eastern Front in early 1944. Seldom did service troops receive proper insulated winter uniforms, because there were simply not enough for the combat troops to go around. (HITM)

FROM RETREAT TO DEFEAT

A MG34 machine gunner can be seen standing inside the cupola of his tank during the winter. In the distance a long column of various modes of transport can be seen stretched out as far as the eye can see. The bulk of the transport is horse-drawn, which was used until then end of the war. (HITM)

Troops wearing reversible winter uniforms lead a horse-drawn sled to the front in early 1944. Wheeled transport was generally useless in the trackless wastes and forests, and often the most effective means of transport was the sled. (HITM)

PART II: WINTER 1943/44–AUTUMN 1944

German paratroopers or Fallschirmjäger with a MG34 machine gun whilst operating on the Eastern Front in 1944. Throughout the war, this band of elite soldiers, often fighting alongside the Army, were seldom used as parachutists, frequently being given tasks that tested their combat abilities to the very limits of skill and endurance. On the Eastern Front they continued to adapt and fight with courage and skill. However even the Fallschirmjäger soon learnt that their fighting ability and audacity were no substitute for superior enemy armour and artillery firepower. (HITM)

In this photograph a MG42 machine gun crew wearing winter reversible uniforms have set-up in a fortified position in order to afford some protection from enemy fire. The machine gunner is firing on long range targets using the optical sight provided to heavy machine-guns. The terms light and heavy machine guns defined the role and not the weight of the gun. The machine gun is being fired from its tripod mount. (HITM)

German troops with a captured Russian Maxim machine gun during the battle of the Cherkassy pocket in early 1944. It was not until 16 February that Hitler finally gave permission for the breakout to begin. Thanks to the sacrifices of 5th SS Division 'Wiking' and SS Sturmbrigade 'Wallonien' almost 32,000 German troops were able to escape almost certain devastation and death in the pocket. (HITM)

Grenadiers hitch a lift on board a column of PzKpfw IVs during the winter of 1944. German troops often rode onboard armoured vehicles in order to reduce the exertion of trudging miles on foot with their equipment. It was also one of the quickest methods of reaching the front lines, or withdrawing units from one battlefront to another. (HITM)

The crew pose for the camera with their Hummel tank destroyer onboard a flatbed railway car. This vehicle is destined for the front lines in 1944. The first Hummels to see action were at Kursk. Thereafter each Panzer division was supposed to have at least one Hummel battery. (HITM)

A group of Panzer officers joke among themselves during winter operations in 1944. Two of the men are wearing the green splinter-pattern German Army camouflage used on heavy reversible winter uniforms, whilst the other men are wearing mouse-grey camouflage versions. The Panzer officer in the centre is a recipient of the Knight's Cross, with Oakleaves and Swords. (HITM)

A Marder II trundles along a road in southern Russia. By March 1944 Army Group had insufficient forces to hold back the Russians and as a consequence many parts of the front lines were burst wide open. German mobile reserves had all been worn down to near-extinction and this began to lead to a number of forces becoming encircled (HITM)

PART II: WINTER 1943/44–AUTUMN 1944

4. The destruction of Army Group Centre

Fighting Strength of the German Army June 1944

Army Group	June	May
North	376,268	350,958
Centre	578,225	499,450
South Ukraine	418,197	360,984
North Ukraine	475,347	423,579

The German Army Group Centre had managed, in spite of the overwhelming enemy superiority, to maintain the strategic initiative on the Eastern Front until the summer of 1943, when Operation Zitadelle, was decisively defeated. Following the defeat, for the next several months the Red Army began a series of powerful offensive operations that consequently compelled Army Group Centre to withdraw westward.

By May 1944 the Army Group had been ground down through a battle of attrition and as a consequence could no longer sustain itself cohesively on the battlefield. For months the German Army had fought desperately to maintain unity and hold their meagre positions, fighting for which often saw thousands of soldiers perish. It now not only lacked sufficient amounts of weapons and equipment but suffered huge shortages of manpower. The heavy drain of powerful Panzer units and other elite forces to the Western Front and north Ukraine had left the centre of the German Eastern Front very weak, without proper armour and aircraft support. In mid-June 1944 Army Group Centre had 34 infantry divisions, two Panzergrenadier divisions, two Luftwaffe field divisions, seven security divisions and just one Panzer division. To the rear were several Hungarian divisions, but these troops were badly understrength and unable to support the main German force for any appreciable length of time. In total the German Army had the equivalent of 52 divisions, with some 420,000 troops, and a further 400,000 in support. Although on paper this was considered to be a substantial force, the German infantry divisions during that summer were stretched beyond their limits. The front line in which the German soldiers were supposed to defend was immense. Each division were supposed to defend a 12–16 mile front, but every mile was on average only protected by 60 frontline infantry, supported by two or three artillery pieces and a handful of assault guns. To make matters worse the quality of these soldiers had declined rapidly through the year, due to the enormous casualties. Since 1943 they were steadily replaced with troops of the Volksdeutsche, and ethnic Germans drafted from Eastern Europe. Although this bolstered the frontline German units, generally neither the Volksdeutsche nor the ethnic Germans were strong enough to withstand powerful Red Army assaults. With combat performance far reduced even the strongest German infantry units were beginning to display low morale. Defeat seemed imminent and yet the Germans were once again spared from total destruction as the Soviet offensive in the centre petered out. The temporary lull gave the German Army enough time to build a number of defensive positions. In the Belorussian sector, for instance, where the front had been relatively static for some months, the Germans feverishly constructed lines of trenches reinforced with machine-gun and mortar pits. There were defensive belts heavily mined, most of them protected by extensive barbed wire barriers and some anti-tank guns.

In spite of the heavily fortified string of defensive lines, the fortifications were still inadequate, especially considering that there were some 1,700,000 Red Army troops and support personnel, more than double their German opponents, all preparing to launch a new massive offensive against Army Group Centre.

On the morning of 22 June 1944, three years to the day since the German Army had begun its campaign on the Eastern Front, the Russians finally unleashed their long-awaited offensive. The codename was 'Operation Bagration', and it opened up with a massive artillery bombardment intended to smash the German defensive positions and annihilate Army Group Centre. The Russian 1st Baltic and 3rd Belorussian Fronts attacked northwest and southeast of the city of Vitebsk. The 3rd Panzer Army was taken completely by surprise. During the course of the day as the German defence lines began to crack under the mighty hammer blows of Russian artillery and attacking armour, the 3rd Panzer Army fought a desperate battle of attrition losing many of its units. The next day the Russians tore through the 3rd Panzer Army and closed its mighty jaws around the smouldering city of Vitebsk. On 24 June the 9th Army, still in a state of confusion from the massive Russian attack, was penetrated by the 1st Belorussian Front near the Beresina. Almost immediately the front begun to collapse under the pressure leaving many units either encircled or totally annihilated. By the end of the fourth day Army Group Centre had committed all its reserves without stemming or even temporarily halting the Soviet drive. Already five German divisions were encircled and Vitebsk almost lost. All over the front confusion swept throughout the German divisions. Other divisions that had not been severely mauled attempted to hold vital lines. The 3rd Panzer Army, for instance, tried desperately to cling to the Dvina and Ulla Rivers fifty miles west of Vitebsk, but could only hold-out for a short period of time. As for the 9th Army, its troops were enduring some of the heaviest ground and aerial attacks that it had ever experienced. Near Bobruisk the situation was critical. Some 40,000 troops were now trapped inside a pocket measuring some 13 miles in diameter east of the city. A series of desperate breakouts were undertaken, but the Russian artillery was so heavy it became a vast killing ground as the Red Army Air Force joined in the slaughter. Even the 12th Panzer Division, which had been hurried from Army Group North, could not help relieve the siege around the city.

By 28 June the 9th Army was almost decimated; 4th Army was in full retreat, and 3rd Panzer Army was penetrated in a number of places and barely able to maintain its forces cohesively. Nevertheless, Hitler was adamant that his troops hold another line of defence, in spite of the appalling casualties already inflicted on the Army Group. In less than a week's fighting the Germans had lost some 70,000 troops killed and captured. Even falling back to another defence line could not prevent the inevitable wholesale destruction of Army Group Centre. By early July most of the Army Group was trapped east of the city of Minsk by advancing Russian columns. The bitter defensive fighting had finally taken its toll and as a consequence Army Group Centre had lost 25 divisions. The 4th Army had suffered terrible losses with some 130,000 lost out of its original strength of 165,000 men. The 3rd Panzer Army lost 10 divisions. The 9th Army was badly shattered along with remnants of the once-powerful 2nd Army. In total 28 divisions with more than 400,000 men were captured. The destruction of Army Group Centre was the greatest single defeat of the German Army of the Second World War. It had suffered a defeat far greater than that of the disaster that had befallen the 6th Army at Stalingrad. As for the Russian Army they were once again victorious. They had covered some 200 miles during the offensive without pause and were now deep in liberated territory ravaged by recent fighting. The successful conclusion of 'Operation Bagration' had effectively sealed the coffin of the German Army in the East. What was left of its mangled and exhausted forces limped westward into Poland to begin a heavy reinforcement of the Vistula River line.

PART II: WINTER 1943/44–AUTUMN 1944

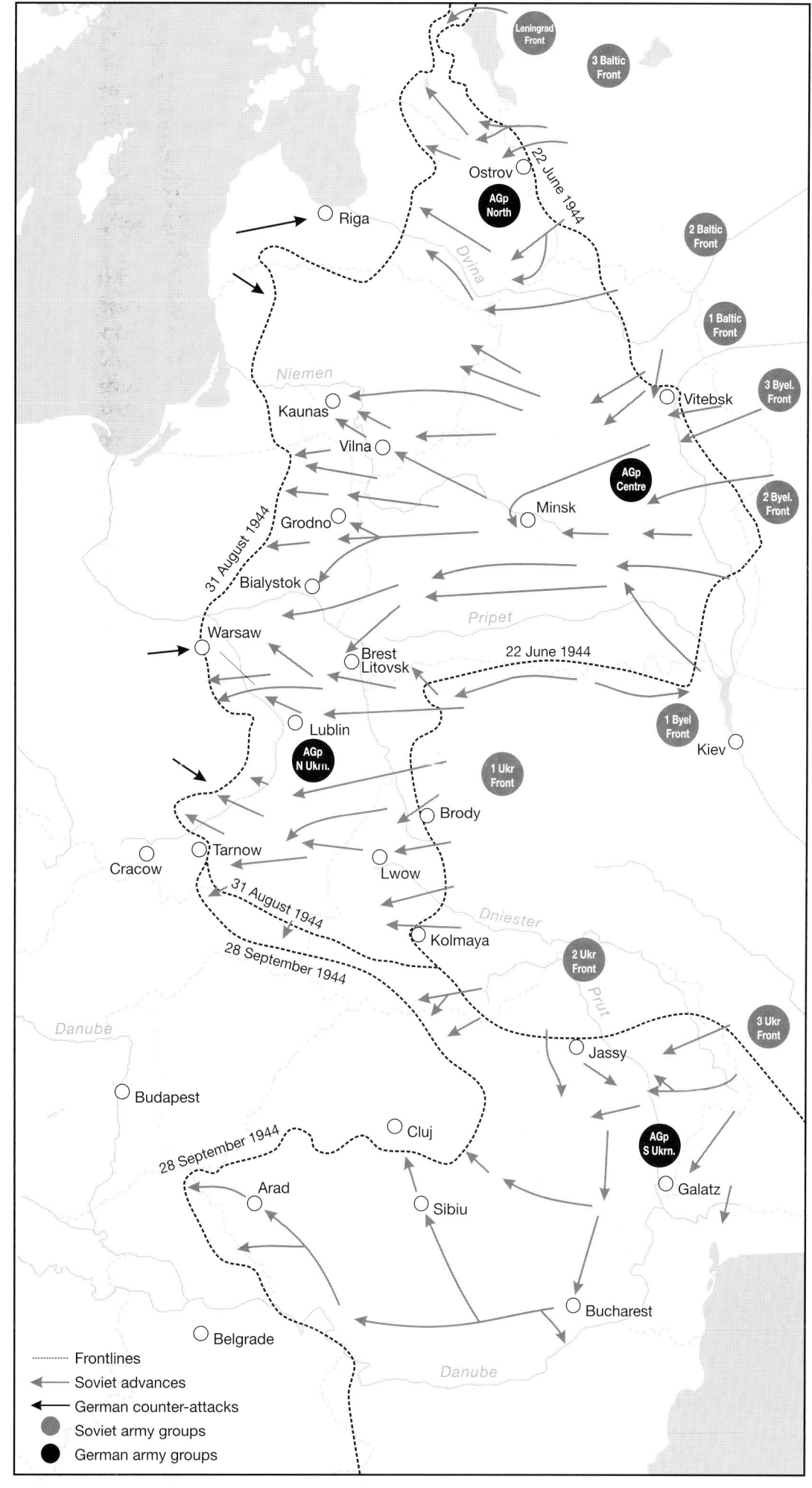

Map 3: Eastern Front, Soviet Summer Offensives 1944

Halftracks towing artillery can be seen being loaded onto flatbed railway cars in March 1944. One of the main factors of the success of the Panzers divisions on the Eastern Front was their speed and mobility to quickly and efficiently transport armour from one battlefront to another, even during withdrawals. (HITM)

Two soldiers pose for the camera whilst standing onboard a railway flatcar, which is transporting much-needed halftracks to the frontlines in late March 1944. The vehicles still retain their winter whitewash paint. In the spring, this paint was to be washed off, exposing the original three-colour summer camouflage scheme. However, by the end of 1944 many crews did not reapply the whitewash due to time and critical shortages of supplies. (HITM)

Armoured vehicles belonging to the 24th Panzer Division are seen moving across uneven terrain in the spring of 1944. There are a multitude of armoured vehicles consisting of halftracks armed with flak guns towing ammunition trailers, Sdkfz 251 halftracks and a Marder III tank destroyer. (HITM)

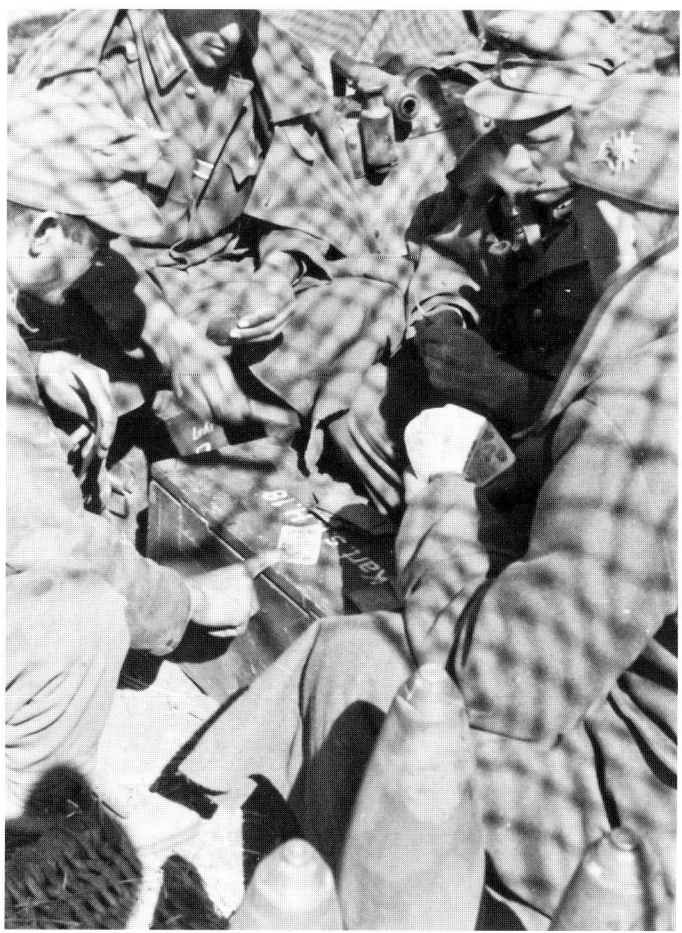

On the southern sector of the Eastern Front a Gebirgsjäger artillery crew are seen playing cards during a brief lull in the fighting in May 1944. By this period of the war the Crimea had been cleared of German forces and strong Soviet troops were now bearing down on the Carpathian Mountains. Romania was then overrun, and the 1st and 5th Gebirgsjäger Divisions were driven back to end the year fighting in Hungary. (HITM)

FROM RETREAT TO DEFEAT

A StuG III Luftwaffe crew take a much-needed respite during operations on the Eastern Front in the summer of 1944. The bulk of the Luftwaffe field divisions served on the Eastern Front and fought under Army command. Losses among the Luftwaffe field divisions were immense, but they continued resisting until the very end of the war. (HITM)

A MG42 machine gunner manning one of the heavily fortified positions during 'Operation Bagration'. For months Army Group Centre had been constructing lines of trenches reinforced with machine guns and mortar pits. In front of these lines there were extensive belts that were heavily mined, and most of them were protected by barbed-wire barriers and a few anti-tank guns. However, these German defences were no match against the mighty Red Army. (HITM)

Grenadiers feverishly mount a StuG III Ausf.G during 'Operation Bagration'. A MG42 machine gun can be seen on top of the assault gun for local defence. Within twenty-four hours of the initial attack the German defence lines begun to crack under the mighty hammer blows of Russian artillery and attacking armour. The Russian offensive was the largest Red Army attack thus far of the war. (HITM)

German anti-tank gunners prepare to use their Pak gun in anger against advancing Russian forces during 'Operation Bagration'. As Soviet forces smashed through the German defences a state of confusion quickly spread among troops of the German Army. By the end of the fourth day of the offensive German forces had committed all their reserves without stemming or even temporarily halting the Russian attack. (HITM)

In this photograph one of the Tiger tanks from the 509th Heavy Panzer Battalion arrives at the front on 1 June 1944 after receiving a full compliment of Tiger Is. The 509th was attached to Army Group Centre and was placed in the line of advance of the Russian offensive. The 509th saw heavy fighting at Novosselki, Shitomir and Chelmik and on 8 September, the Battalion lost sixteen Tigers within twenty-fours hours near Kielce in Poland. (HITM)

Troops from the 256th Infatry Division are seen here manning a defensive position near Orsha on 23 June 1944. Along the entire front soldiers from the division tried their best to delay the Red Army from breaking through, but commanders were soon compelled to order their units to fall back to more defensible positions. (HITM)

PART II: WINTER 1943/44–AUTUMN 1944

A rapid command conference in the field, July 1944. The commander of a Sturmgeschütz unit gives orders to his men – the strain of combat is clearly visible. Note the MP44 assault rifle in the foreground. (Ullstein Bilderdienst)

By early July 1944 almost the entire force of Army Group Centre had been decimated. Those units lucky enough to escape the pending slaughter hurriedly moved westward. Here in this photograph infantry withdraw along with a mid-production Tiger I from the 509th Heavy Panzer Battalion. (HITM)

Infantry withdraw west past burning buildings following the annihilation of Army Group Centre. In total 17 German divisions were utterly destroyed, and over 50 other divisions were severely damaged. The Russian summer offensive in June 1944 had undoubtedly brought about the worst defeat of the German Army throughout the Second World War. (HITM)

A soldier scours the sky from his well-camouflaged SdKfz 251 armoured radio carrier. For local defence the halftrack is armed with a MG42 machine gun. Foliage was applied over most armoured vehicles during the last years of the war. This was generally done to make it more difficult for the enemy to identify equipment. The foliage was also used to break up or alter the shape of the equipment, since much of Russia, especially in the south, consisted of large flat plains and open fields, which provided limited amounts of cover. (HITM)

Two German soldiers run to take up another defensive position whilst in action on the Eastern Front in July 1944. In spite of the virtual decimation of Army Group Centre the German Army still managed to temporarily slow down the Russian onslaught. Throughout July remnants from Army Group Centre withdrew steadily through Poland, much of the force being driven back towards Kaunas, the Neman River and Bialystok. (HITM)

Mountain troops of 3rd Gebirgsjäger Division struggle to pull an anti-tank gun through dense undergrowth during operations in south Ukraine. Since the spring of 1944 the division had formed part of the new 6th Army where it served until October with the Hungarian IX Corps, which was fighting in Hungary. (HITM)

An artillery tractor armed with a flak gun in a field during the late summer of 1944. Although these vehicles were primarily designed as a light anti-aircraft gun, both the 2cm and 3.7cm flak guns were very useful in engaging ground targets. In the distance 15cm howitzers can be seen positioned for action. (HITM)

PART II: WINTER 1943/44–AUTUMN 1944

5. Defending Poland

By incredible efforts and courageous fighting the German Army managed to slow down the Russian offensive on the central sector of the Eastern Front. Throughout July Army Group Centre was withdrawing steadily through Poland. Its weary soldiers had been forced back towards Kaunas, the Neman River and Bialystok. The last of the German infantry units capable of retreating along the Warsaw highway over the Vistula at Siedlce was undertaken and assisted by the crack Waffen-SS division Totenkopf and the Luftwaffe's Hermann Goring Division. The whole German position in the East was now cracking, and any hope of repairing it was made almost impossible by crippling shortages of troops. German infantry divisions continued desperately trying to fill the dwindling ranks. However, by the end of July the Red Army was already making good progress towards the Polish capital, Warsaw. On 7 August 1944 the Soviet offensive finally came to a halt east of Warsaw. Feldmarschall Model sent Hitler a optimistic report telling him that Army Group Centre had finally set up a continuous front from the south of Shaulyay to the right boundary on the River Vistula near Pulawy. The new front itself in Poland stretched some 420 miles and was manned by thirty-nine divisions and brigades. Although the amount of strength seemed impressive the German Army was actually weak and thinly-stretched. What made matters worse was the fact it faced a Russian force that was a third of the total Red Army strength. With these understrength divisions, the Germans were compelled to hold large areas along the Vistula River, which included Warsaw. To the Germans Warsaw possessed great strategic importance due to the vital traffic arteries running north-south and east-west, which crossed into the city. The Germans were therefore determined, if they hoped to keep control of the Eastern Front, to hold onto the city at all costs.

As news reached Waraw that the Russians were approaching, the Polish Home Army rose against the German forces, in what became known as the Warsaw Uprising. In the north of the city the 4th and 19th Panzer Divisions together with the Herman Goring Division saw extensive action in trying to repulse the uprising. Whilst the fighting raged inside the capital, north of the city Soviet troops had already made some impressive gains by pushing the 2nd Army towards the Narew River. Fortunately for the German troops the Red Army were too exhausted and the offensive ground to a halt.

But the lull in Poland was not mirrored elsewhere. In the north, Soviet forces were already in East Prussia threatening the German forces in that area by reaching the Baltic and cutting off Army Group North. In southern Poland the 1st Ukrainian Front captured Lemberg, while Romania fell to the 2nd and 3rd Ukrainian Fronts. Soviet forces had also penetrated Hungary and its powerful armoured forces soon reached the capital, Budapest. On 20 August, the 2nd Ukrainian Front broke through powerful German defences, and the Red Army reached the Bulgarian border on 1 September. Within a week, Soviet troops arrived along the Yugoslav frontier. On 8 September, Bulgaria and Romania then declared war on Germany. It seemed that nothing but a series of defeats now plagued the German Army during the summer of 1944.

In a radical effort to stem the series of reverses, General Heinz Guderian, Chief of the General staff, proposed that thirty divisions of Army Group North, which were redundant in Kurland, be shipped back to the Homeland so they could be re-supplied and re-strengthened to reinforce Army Group Centre in Poland. Hitler, however, emphatically refused Guderian's proposal. As a consequence of Hitler's negative response, as predicted, by October Army Group North was cut off leaving 4th Army with only four weak corps to defend East Prussia against the full might of the Soviet forces.

In Army Group Centre the 3rd Panzer Army and 4th Army were holding tenaciously to a weak salient in the north, while to the southwest, along the Narew River the 2nd Army was still holding the river line. Army Group A had dug a string of defences from Modlin to Kaschau, with the 9th Army positioned either side of Warsaw along the Vistula. The 4th Panzer Army had dug-in at Baranov and was holding positions against strong Russian attacks. The 17th Army had fortified its positions with a string of machine-gun posts and mines between the Vistula and the Beskides, whilst the 1st Panzer Army was holding the area of Kaschau and Jaslo.

For the remaining weeks of 1944 the German Army defended Poland with everything it could muster. The fighting withdrawal had been a gruelling battle of attrition for those German divisions fortunate enough to escape the slaughter and build new defences in Poland. The bulk of the forces left to defend the frontlines were exhausted and undermanned. With reserves almost non-existent the dwindling ranks were bolstered by old men and low-grade troops. Struggling to find more manpower, convalescents and the medically unfit, known as 'stomach and 'ear' battalions because most men were hard of hearing or suffered from ulcers, were also drafted into the ranks. Poland it seemed would be defended at all costs, despite the age and quality of the soldiers that manned the lines.

This 3.7cm Flak anti-aircraft gun, mounted on the back of an artillery tractor, is supporting ground forces during fighting in Poland in the summer of 1944. By the middle of the war many flak guns had already joined the flak arsenal of the German Army. Mechanised formations had become well equipped with flak guns, and divisions also had additional anti-aircraft platoons and companies in their Panzergrenadier, Panzer and artillery regiments. (HITM)

A well camouflaged SdKfz 234/2 Puma. This eight-wheeled armoured car is armed with a long barrelled 5cm KwK L/60 gun in a fully revolving turret. These vehicles were used by both the German Army and Waffen-SS in armoured reconnaissance battalions, where they quickly acquitted themselves well. The success of this particular variant led to another version being produced known as the SdKfz 234/3, which was armed with a powerful 7.5cm KwK L/24 low velocity gun. (HITM)

PART II: WINTER 1943/44–AUTUMN 1944

Troops of the Fallschirm-Panzer-Division 1. Hermann Göring (1st Parachute-Panzer-Division Hermann Göring) being inspected by officers of the division in Poland. During the first half of 1944 the division had been fighting in Italy, but on 15 July it was ordered out of the line to prepare for transport to the Eastern Front.
The division arrived at the Vistula front in mid-September and was immediately thrown into action, fighting alongside the veteran 5th SS Panzer Division Wiking on the Vistula River between Modlin and Warsaw. (HITM)

Officers inspecting a unit of the Panzer-Division Hermann Göring. A StuG III Ausf.G assault gun can be seen to the right of the photograph. During the summer of 1944, a number of veteran cadres were drawn from the division for the formation of Fallschirm-Panzergrenadier-Division 2 Hermann Göring, the division's sister formation being formed in Radom Poland. As a result the bulk of the division's supply units were removed, as were many of its staff officers. These units were to assist in the creation of what would be known on the battlefield as the Parachute-Panzer-Corps Hermann Göring, under which the two Hermann Göring divisions were to operate together. (HITM)

During the same inspection officers can be seen standing next to a StuG III of the Hermann Göring Division. Within weeks of its arrival in the East it was decided that the division was to be attached to the newly formed Army Group Vistula, then defending the Polish capital, Warsaw. (HITM)

A SdKfz 234/2 Puma eight-wheeled reconnaissance vehicle parked on a training ground. Two crewmembers can be seen with the vehicle. Apart from being armed with a 5cm gun the Puma is also fitted with smoke candle dischargers that can be seen fitted to the side of the traversing turret. Next to the SdKfz 234/2 is a SdKfz 234/3 variant mounting the 7.5cm KwK L/24. (HITM)

PART II: WINTER 1943/44–AUTUMN 1944

Three photographs taken minutes apart showing officers inspecting a unit from the Hermann Göring division as it simulates battle conditions prior to its deployment with Army Group Vistula in October 1944. The Parachute-Panzer-Corps Hermann Göring was activated in early October 1944, and the Hermann Göring Panzer division, along with its sister Panzergrenadier division, was transferred to the command of the corps. (HITM)

FROM RETREAT TO DEFEAT

Two photographs showing Luftwaffe troops from the Hermann Göring division lining up for inspection. A StuG III can be seen halted on a track behind the officers. In October, as the situation in the north deteriorated, the Panzer Corps was transferred to East Prussia to halt the Soviet offensive which had already cut off Army Group North in what became known as the Kurland Pocket. The Panzer Corps was involved in heavy defensive fighting near Gumbinnen, and when the Soviet assault petered out in late November, this elite Panzer corps set up a strong defensive position. Over the coming weeks a number of breakout attempts were undertaken with many casualties. The situation became so dire that the Panzer Corps were compelled to be evacuated by sea to Swinemünde in Pomerania. Once it arrived it resumed vicious fighting, defending the Oder-Niesse line against strong Red Army attacks through mid-March 1945. To bolster the corps' strength, the elite Panzergrenadier-Division *Brandenburg* was attached to the unit. (HITM)

Luftwaffe troops belonging to the Hermann Göring Division in Poland during the summer of 1944, gather around a StuG III to listen to encouraging words from their commander. The Hermann Göring Division fought hard on the Eastern Front and as a consequence for their courage and determination the casualties they sustained were huge. (HITM)

Two members of a StuG III crew belonging to the Herman Göring Division pose for the camera whilst sitting on top of their vehicle during the summer of 1944. Elements of the HG units fought with distinction at *Festung* Graudenz in February 1945. During the fighting in the East, Heinrich Göring, the nephew of the Reichsmarschall, was killed in action. (HITM)

The crew of a PzKpfw IV are trying to work out with the aid of a map their next move. This photograph was taken in Poland during the summer of 1944. By August the German front in Poland stretched some 420 miles and was manned by thirty-nine divisions and brigades. With these forces the German Army were compelled to hold large areas along the Vistula, nevertheless in many areas the front line was undermanned. (HITM)

Two armoured vehicles, seen here on a road, which both saw active service on the front lines during the last year of the war. A Jagdpanzer 38(t) Hetzer tank destroyer with several German soldiers sitting atop the vehicle is passing by a PzKpfw V Panther. It was not until July 1944 that the first tank hunting battalions began to be equipped with the Hetzer. These vehicles were primarily used to harass and defend against formations of much larger enemy tanks before retreating. (HITM)

PART II: WINTER 1943/44–AUTUMN 1944

A StuG III Ausf.G variant moves along a dusty road whilst operating along the Vistula River in August 1944. The German Army now defended Poland with everything it could muster. The country was the last bastion before the Reich and each soldier was exhorted to fight to the last man. All available armour, artillery and manpower were moved along the Vistula to fight a gruelling battle of attrition against powerful Soviet forces. (HITM)

A Panther tank, accompanied by grenadiers from the elite 'Grossdeutschland' Division in action in Poland, summer 1944. Note the foliage attached to the men's steel helmets, and the zimmerit anti-magnetic mine paste applied to the Panther. (Ullstein Bilderdienst)

Half-tracks and infantry from the Grossdeutschland Division assembled for a counter-attack in Poland, summer 1944. The vehicles and field positions are liberally camouflaged to prevent detection from the air. (Ullstein Bilderdienst)

In spite of the crippling shortages the German Army fought extremely well in Poland and managed to win a number of defensive battles. In this photograph German troops are escorting Russian prisoners along a road to a fate that can only be imagined. The soldier leading the column is part of the Feldgendarmerie and can be seen wearing the distinctive duty gorget, which gave this arm of service the nickname 'chain dogs'. The Feldgendarmerie were a military body within the German Army and were responsible for a number of police duties, one of them being evacuating prisoners. (HITM)

PART II: WINTER 1943/44–AUTUMN 1944

A halftrack towing an 8.8cm flak gun withdraws across a Polish river during the summer of 1944. The 8.8cm flak gun was used extensively by the German Army throughout the war and it was specifically designed for a dual role and thus possessed a genuine anti-tank capability. (HITM)

German troops from Army Group North interrogate Russian prisoners following a series of successful heavy engagements along the frontier of East Prussia where staunch German defences helped to halt the Russian onslaught. In late 1944 the German front line ran from the Kurischen Haff in the north along the frontier of East Prussia, south-westwards along the Narev River as far as Modlin, near Warsaw, and the continued along the Vistula's western bank to Pulavy. The line then proceeded downriver to Twolen, down the Vistula to Baranov, south-westwards to Kaschau and thence to Hungary. (HITM)

FROM RETREAT TO DEFEAT

A signals post somewhere on the frontline at the end of October 1944. Even by this late period of the war rapid transmission of orders via radio and the fast action taken in response to them were the keys to the success of the German Army maintaining its position cohesively on the front line. The equipment issued to signals units varied considerably from field telephone sets, to ten-line subscriber networks and teleprinters, as well as transmitters and receivers. (HITM)

Anti-tank gunners in a field have camouflaged their Pak gun with heavy foliage during operations in Poland in September or October 1944. The Pak gun provided the German Army with not only effective fire support but also defensive staying power as troops found themselves confronted by ever increasing numbers of enemy tanks. (HITM)

Reserves arrive, ready to be marched off to the front in order to help bolster the already exhausted and undermanned front line troops. With reserves almost non-existent by this stage of the war dwindling ranks were replenished with old men and low-grade troops. The medically unfit, known as 'stomach' and 'ear' battalions, were hastily drafted to help reduce the manpower shortages. (HITM)

From a dug out position in Poland in October 1944 two officers can be seen wearing the green splinter Army reversible camouflage winter uniform. Behind the soldiers are a pile of stick grenades and Panzerfausts. During this period the 3rd Panzer Army and 4th Army were holding in the north while to the southwest, along the Narev River, the 2nd Army was fiercely contesting every foot of ground. Army Group 'A' held the area from Modlin to Kaschau, with 9th Army on either side of Warsaw. The 4th Panzer Army held positions against strong Russian attacks at Baranov, whilst the 17th Army had meanwhile dug in between the Vistula and the Beskides. 1st Panzer Army was trying its best to regroup forces and hold the area around Kaschau and Jaslo. (HITM)

Captured at the moment of firing, the crew of a camouflaged 21cm Mrs18 fires a round miles into the enemy lines. The sound of the massive blast as the projectile leaves the barrel is so loud that the crew protect their ears. They are all wearing the green splinter Army reversible camouflage winter uniforms. (HITM)

A battery of well camouflaged 'Wespe' self-propelled guns open fire against enemy positions in early autumn 1944. This vehicle was armed with a 10.5cm leFH 18/2 L/28 gun and protected by a light armoured superstructure mounted on a chassis of a PzKpfw II tank. The 'Wespe' served in armoured artillery battalions but were lightly armoured, and as a result many of them were lost in battle. (HITM)

From a dugout a soldier scours the terrain ahead using a pair of binoculars. During the last weeks of 1944 the German Army was still fighting on foreign soil. Exhausted and demoralised skeletal units that had been waging a battle of attrition in Poland were now fully aware of the impending defeat that would soon see them fighting in front of the Reich capital, Berlin. (HITM)

In spite of the dire problems facing the German Army smiling soldiers can be seen posing for the camera in their halftrack during the winter of 1944 in Poland. By this period of the war the bulk of the German forces had withdrawn west across the Vistula. Virtually all reserves were gone. The Panzerwaffe was now a shadow of its former self. What was left of the armour was now loosely organized in ad hoc groups, often piecemeal. As logistical problems intensified, many tanks and assault guns were rendered useless with insufficient fuel. Consequently, in a number of sectors crews were compelled to abandon their tracked or wheeled vehicles and move either on foot or by horse transport. The last months of the war had become desperate days for the German Army. (HITM)

PART III

Winter 1944/45–May 1945

6. Army in Retreat

The year of 1944 ended with the German Army still fighting on foreign soil trying desperately to gain the initiative and throw the Red Army back from its remorseless drive on the German frontier. But despite the skill and determination shown by the German soldiers in late 1944, most of them were aware that 1945 would be the fateful year, the year of decision.

In January 1945 along the Vistula Front hope dawned among some of the more fanatical commanders of the German Army. The strongest of the forces deployed along the Vistula against the Russians were in Army Group Centre. Its battle line ran more than 350 miles. However, each division that was placed on the front lines was perilously understrength and would not be able to contain a Russian attack for any appreciable length of time.

On 13 January 1945 the Soviet offensive opened up and soldiers and Panzer crews from the 4th Panzer Army bore the brunt of the attack on the Vistula. Almost immediately the army was engulfed in a storm of fire. Across the snow-covered terrain Red Army troops and massive amounts of armoured vehicles flooded the battlefield. By the end of the first day the battle had ripped open a breach more than twenty miles wide in the Vistula Front. The 4th Panzer Army was virtually annihilated. Small groups of German soldiers tried frantically to fight their way westwards through the Red flood of infantry and tanks.

As the whole German military campaign in the East began collapsing it was proposed that all German forces located between the Oder and Vistula rivers be amalgamated into a new army group named 'Army Group Vistula'. SS Reichsführer Heinrich Himmler was to command the new army group. German soldiers together with elite formations of the Waffen-SS were supposed to prevent the Soviets from breaking through. However, the once-mighty German Army was now suffering from an unmistakable lack of provisions. By January 1945, the problems had become so critical that even children and old men were being thrown into what was now being called the last bastion of defence for the Reich. In Army Group Vistula the German Army could no longer function properly. There was no contact between units on the battlefield, battalions were out of touch with their companies, and regiments had no link with their divisions. Successive blows by the Red Army began to tear apart Himmler's Army Group and send scattered German formations reeling back westward towards the Oder or northwestwards into Pomerania. As the whole front began withdrawing both the 9th Army and 2nd Army's right wing lost contact with each other. In a drastic measure to restore the disintegrating situation General Weiss, commanding the 2nd Army, tried to stabilize the front on the Vistula between the town of Thorn and Graudenz. But still Soviet forces were overwhelming many German positions and pushing back Hitler's exhausted forces.

Despite the best efforts of the German Army to bolster its dwindling ranks on the Eastern Front, nothing could now mask the fact that they were dwarfed by the superiority of the Red Army. It was estimated that the Russians had some six million men along a front which stretched from the Adriatic to the Baltic. To the German soldiers facing the Russians, the outcome was almost certain death. They were well aware that what they had done in Russia and the occupied territories had caused the Red Army to exact a terrible revenge. One German grenadier wrote:

> You did not need just to fear the Russian offensive, Nazi leaders had made it clear with promises as well as threats of execution of anyone who deserted or retreated without orders.

As the Nazi empire was sheared off piece by piece, Dr Josef Goebbels, the Reich's propaganda chief, begun to switch from terror mongering to reassuring the population that victory was just around the corner. However, in an atmosphere of near-panic created by refugees and their stories of atrocities by the Russians, there was little to console them. Many stories had already reached the German front lines as to how the Red Army had raped and murdered women. The widespread panic among the civilians was causing the German command many problems, especially with supply and troop movements. In some areas the roads had become so congested with civilians and soldiers that it brought many miles of the road network to a complete standstill.

Out on the battlefield, the realization among troops that they might lose the war was seldom admitted openly. But most of the soldiers already knew that the end would come soon. Troops were not convinced by their commander's encouragements especially when they were lying in their trenches subjected to hours of bombardment by guns that never seemed to lack shells. Poorly armed and undermanned, infantry and Panzer divisions were exhausted shadows of their former selves. Although there were shortages in everything, the ordinary German soldier did not need any propaganda to urge him on.

The last great offensives that brought the Russians their final victory in Eastern Europe began during the third week of January 1945. Marshal Konev's 1st Ukrainian Front surged into Silesia after the capture of Radom and Krakow. On the night of 27 January, the German divisions of the 17th Army pulled out of the region towards the Oder River. The principle objective of the Red Army during late January 1945 was for an all-out assault along the Baltic to crush the remaining under-strength German units that had formed Army Group North. It was these heavy, sustained attacks that eventually restricted the German-held territory in the north-east to a few small pockets of land surrounding three ports: Libau in Kurland, Pillau in East Prussia and Danzig at the mouth of River Vistula. It was here along the Baltic that the German defenders attempted to stall the massive Russian onslaught with the few weapons and men they had at their disposal. Every German soldier defending the area was aware of the significance if it were captured. Not only would the coastal garrisons be cut off and eventually destroyed, but also masses of civilian refugees would be prevented from escaping from the ports by sea. Terrified civilians eager to board the next ships to the homeland queued night and day until the next vessel came in. They were so desperate to leave that they stood out in the open, enduring constant bombing and strafing by low-flying Russian aircraft, whose presence was now unchallenged in the sky.

For the next several weeks thousands of civilians risked their lives in order to escape from the clutches of the Red Army. Even by the end of March 1945, as Soviet troops fought their way into the outskirts of Gdynia, the German Navy continued rescuing many refugees before the Russians could get to them first. German soldiers too, even remnants of elite Waffen-SS units, found themselves faced with a similar experience. Thousands of dishevelled troops streamed towards the coast, mingling with countless numbers of terrified women and children. Just along the coast in Danzig, the Russians stormed the ancient Teutonic city, smashing into the rear of fleeing German troops who were making their way desperately along the Vistula estuary. To the German soldiers that saw Danzig fall, it marked a complete disaster along the Baltic. Russian soldiers, however, saw Danzig as a way of exterminating Teutonic culture, which had long since been despised. All over the city, they blew up old buildings, set alight churches and randomly executed groups of soldiers that had not raised the white flag of surrender, but had fought on until they ran out of ammunition.

Elsewhere along the Baltic coast isolated areas of German resistance continued to fight on, but still they had no prospect of holding back the Russians. Hitler made it quite clear that Army Group Kurland was not to be evacuated. To the Führer, Kurland was the last bastion of defence in the East and every soldier, he said, was to 'stand and fight' and wage an unprecedented battle of attrition. In fact, what Hitler had done in a single sentence was to condemn to death some 8,000 officers and more than 181,000 soldiers and Luftwaffe personnel. Those soldiers who managed to escape the destruction of Army Group Kurland retreated back towards the River Oder or returned by ship to Germany.

On other parts of the Eastern Front fighting was merciless, with both sides imposing harsh measures on their men to stand where they were and fight to the death. In the city of Breslau, these same measures were also being applied to the German Army. Since September 1944, Hitler had appreciated the importance of holding the city of Breslau from the approaching Red Army and declared it a fortress. As with other towns and villages lining the approaches to the Homeland, Breslau's infantry formations consisted mainly of old men and young boys who were poorly-equipped and hastily trained for combat. Yet four months later in January 1945, the city was still poised for the arrival of the Russians. By February, the sound of approaching Russian guns brought the city to panic stations. It was the 269th Infantry Division, withdrawing in the face of the massive Soviet advance that was given the principle objective of forming the main defence of Breslau.

The Red Army drive was so powerful and swift that by 14 February the city was cut off and isolated, miles behind the Russian front. To test the defenders of Breslau, the Red Army launched a series of probing attacks into the city. Four Soviet divisions then carried out a furious assault that penetrated Breslau's defences. Volkssturm, Hitlerjugend, Waffen-SS and various formations from the 269th Infantry Division put up a staunch defence with every available weapon they could muster. As the battle raged, both German soldiers and civilians were cut to pieces by Russian fire. During these vicious battles, which continued into May 1945, after Berlin had fallen, there were many acts of courageous fighting. Cheering and yelling, old men and boys of the Volkssturm and Hitlerjugend advanced across open terrain into a heavy barrage of machine gun and mortar fire. By the first week of March, Russian infantry had driven back the defenders into the inner city and were pulverising it street by street. Lightly-clad Volkssturm and Hitlerjugend were still resisting, forced to fight in the sewers beneath the ravaged city. Almost 60,000 Russian soldiers were killed or wounded trying to capture the city, with some 29,000 German military and civilian casualties. When Breslau finally capitulated, the Red Army was bitter at its extended defence and vented its anger against the civilians.

As the massive Russian forces pushed ever westward, the German Army along with the Waffen-SS, Luftwaffe, Volkssturm and Hitlerjugend formations withdrew under increasing pressure nearer and nearer to the Homeland. With every defeat and withdrawal came ever-increasing pressure on the commanders to exert harsher discipline on their weary men. The thought of fighting on German soil for the first time resulted in mixed feelings among the men. Although the defence of the Reich automatically stirred emotional feelings to fight for their land, many soldiers were quite openly aware that morale was being completely destroyed. They had all received a message from the Führer telling them to fight to the death, but they no longer had the manpower resources or strength to wage such a bloody war of attrition. More young conscripts began showing signs that they did not want to die for a lost cause. Conditions on the Eastern Front were miserable not only for the newest recruit, but also the battle-hardened veteran who had survived many months of bitter conflict against the Red Army. The cold harsh weather during February and March prevented the soldiers digging trenches more than a few feet down. But the main problems that confronted the German Army during this period of the war were shortages of ammunition, fuel and vehicles. Some vehicles in the divisions could only be used in an emergency and troops were strictly prohibited from using them without permission from the commanding officer. The daily ration on average per division was for two shells per gun.

With such drastic restrictions of every kind, thousands of under-nourished civilians, mostly women, alongside remaining slave labourers, were marched out to expend all their available energy to dig lines of anti-tank ditches in a drastic attempt to hold back the Russian armoured force.

For the benefit of the newsreel camera, which was intended somehow to help bolster the morale of the troops, Hitler made a secret visit on 13 March 1945 to the Oder Front. In fact, Hitler did not meet one ordinary soldier at the front and was surrounded by well-armed SS guards. During his brief war conference on the terrible situation faced by his Army, he gave a formal speech on the necessity of holding the positions. He told General Busse, commander of the 9th Army, to use all available weapons and equipment at his disposal to hold back the Russians. However, nothing could stop the Red Army's drive.

Out on the Vistula Front, German troops were now barely holding their wavering positions that ran some 175 miles from the Baltic coast to the juncture of the Oder and Neisse in Silesia. Most of the front was now held on the western bank of the Oder. In the north, the ancient city of Stettin, and in the south, the town of Küstrin, were both vital holding points against the main Russian objective of the war – Berlin.

By late March, the situation in Army Group Vistula had become much worse. Not only were supplies dwindling, rations too were becoming so low that some soldiers were beginning to starve. In the ranks where rations were more abundant, most days each soldier received an Army loaf and some stew or soup, which was often cold and not very appetising. The main problem was the lack of clean drinking water. As a result, many of the soldiers suffered from dysentery.

The bulk of the Vistula front was manned by inexperienced training units. Some soldiers were so young that in their rations they were handed sweets instead of tobacco. More experienced soldiers observed that the Soviets were actually playing with them like 'cat and mouse'. Sitting in their trenches constantly cowering under the constant Soviet shelling, almost all of the men seemed overwhelmed by one thing, 'the order to hurry up and retreat'.

Despite all its weaknesses on the Vistula Front, the German Army could still be a formidable opponent. Both young and old alike fought together to hold some kind of line in the face of the massive Russian onslaught. But as soon as the Russians appeared discipline seemed to collapse and panic and confusion swept the lines.

PART III: WINTER 1944/45–MAY 1945

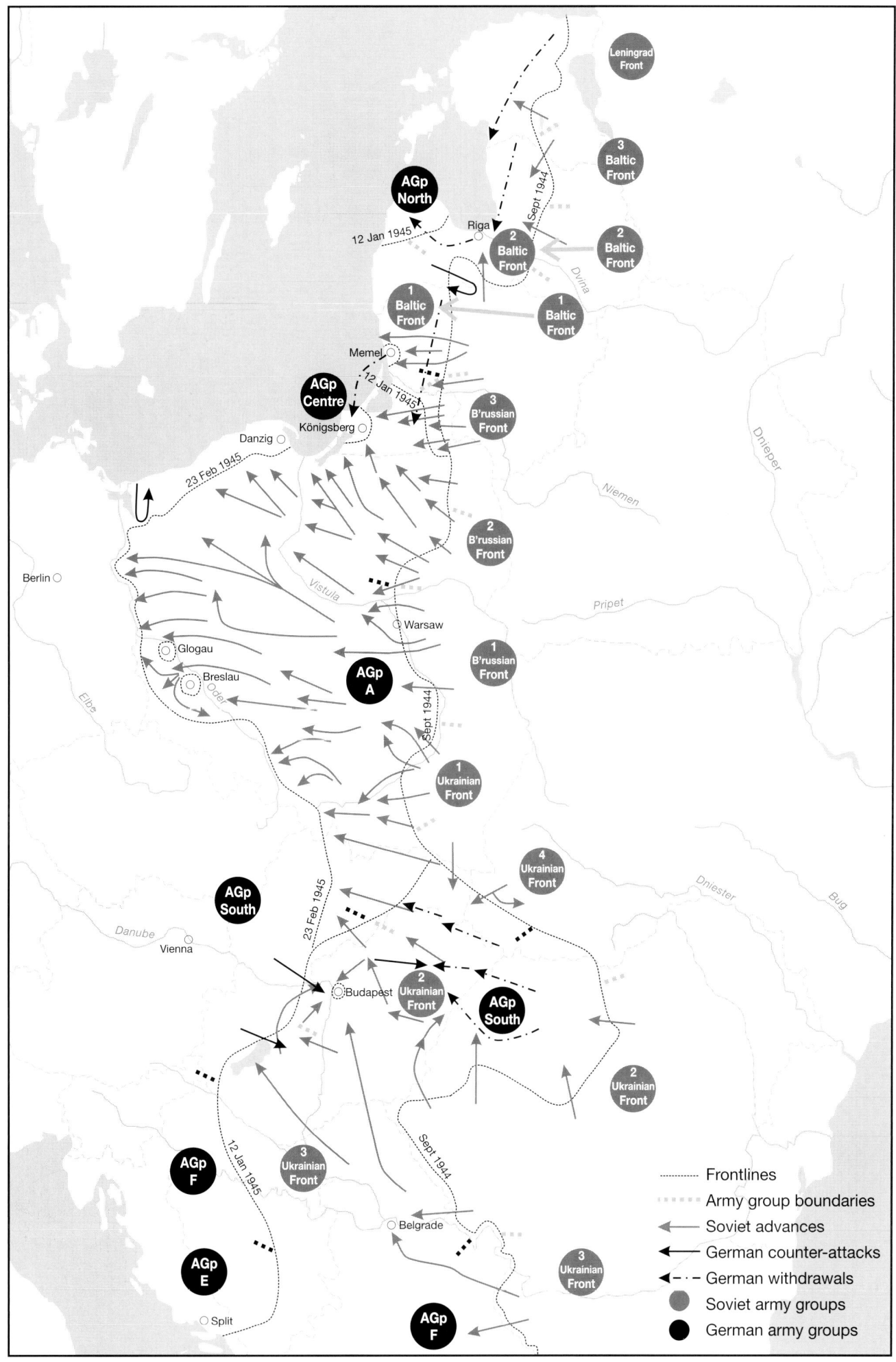

Map 4: Eastern Front, the Soviet drive through Europe 1944-45

Officers confer wearing winter reversibles during the Polish campaign in early January 1945. These soldiers are from the 3rd Panzer Army. The 3rd Panzer Army was part of Army Group Centre, which had its front line along the Vistula that ran nearly 375 miles. In the north stood the 3rd Panzer Army, in the centre the 4th Army and in the south the 2nd Army. (HITM)

An SdKfz 234/1 'Puma' halts inside a town. This heavy eight-wheeled armoured car was purposely built to endure the harsh, rugged conditions on the Eastern Front. This particular early variant is armed with a 2cm cannon, which was totally unsuited to anti-tank combat conditions by 1945. (HITM)

PART III: WINTER 1944/45–MAY 1945

At a maintenance depot a late variant StuG III assault gun can be seen with crew. The StuG is parked next to a Jagdpanzer.IV tank destroyer. These vehicles were built as an improved version of the StuG III, which they were designed to replace. With spaced appliqué plates on the rear superstructure sides and armoured side skirts, its well-sloped body was able to maximise shot deflection. The vehicle was used primarily as an anti-tank weapon. (HITM)

Standing in the snow soldiers from Army Group Centre pose for the camera next to a dwindling supply of 10.5cm howitzers. In Poland Army Group Centre was dangerously understrength and faced an overwhelming enemy army. The Red Army had a numerical superiority of 11 to 1 in infantry, 7 to 1 in armour and a massive 20 to 1 in artillery. (HITM)

A light Horch cross-country vehicle has become stuck in snow and troops are trying to dig out the four-wheeled vehicle. During the last few months of the war transportation for the German Army had become a serious problem with limited fuel stocks. In fact the crisis had become so bad that heavy tanks were being abandoned for lack of fuel. Troops were often compelled to move from one part of the disintegrating to another on foot, trudging miles in deep snow and sometime becoming completely overrun by fast-moving armoured enemy formations. (HITM)

A Gebirgsjäger officer shows off his 'kill' of two animals. Apart from the standard army issue greatcoat he is wearing the fur-covered cap. These winter caps were widely issued to troops serving on the Eastern Front from 1943. (HITM)

PART III: WINTER 1944/45–MAY 1945

A pensive-looking group of German grenadiers awaiting orders to begin a counter-attack, in the Kurland pocket, February 1945. (Ullstein Bilderdienst)

A convoy of German vehicles pass a knocked out Russian 152mm M1937 howitzer during the early winter of 1945. From 1944 onwards the Red Army also mounted the gun on the massive ISU-152 heavy assault gun, which was extensively used against tanks, concrete bunkers and other defensive positions. (HITM)

German troops wearing the standard issue greatcoat and winter camouflage smocks are receiving some supplies for their defensive position. Two Polish children can be seen, which probably suggests that the wooden hut-like dwelling was perhaps their home. It was no uncommon for German forces to commandeer civilian homes. In fact, some families still lived on the site whilst German troops operated, as this photograph suggests. (HITM)

Gebirgsjäger ski-troops march along a snow-covered road wearing white camouflage smocks. The standard winter clothing worn was the padded winter suit. This was a heavy padded double-breasted jacket with hood attached. It was reversible, with grey or camouflage pattern on one side and white on the other. With this jacket were worn a pair of matching trousers. Most troops wore the winter smocks for many months on end and as a consequence they became extremely dirty. (HITM)

PART III: WINTER 1944/45–MAY 1945

Troops queuing to receive their meagre rations from a makeshift mobile field kitchen in January 1945. By this time soldiers were becoming increasingly undernourished due to the severe lack of rations. The basic ration for the men was an army loaf and some stew or soup, which was often cold and unappetising. (HITM)

In Poland a soldier can be seen repairing a punctured tyre. One of the greatest hazards of travelling in the East was the lack of good-quality roads for vehicles. Wheeled vehicles in particular suffered immeasurable problems due to bad road surfaces. It was not uncommon for vehicles to get punctures almost on a weekly basis. If the vehicle did not breakdown due to a puncture, it was invariably prone to frequent mechanical problems due to the endless distances which the vehicle had to travel without any proper maintenance. By 1945, fuel had become the main cause of vehicle breakdowns in the German Army. (HITM)

This atmospheric photograph shows reinforcements marching towards the front through a snowstorm, East Prussia, January 1945. The German infantry ended the war as it had begun it, travelling the majority of its distances on foot. (Ullstein Bilderdienst)

Two officers on horseback wearing the German Army splinter green winter reversible in late January 1945. On 25 January 1945, Hitler renamed the three Eastern Front Army Groups. Army Group North became Army Group Kurland; Army Group Centre became Army Group North and Army Group A became Army Group Centre. By the end of January overwhelming Russian forces had secured bridgeheads over the frozen Oder, 300 miles west from their starting point. However, due to logistical problems aggravated by the spring thaw, the lack of air support, and fear of encirclement through flank attacks from East Prussia, Pomerania and Silesia, the Red Army temporarily ground to a halt. But, the coming of the storm was near. (HITM)

PART III: WINTER 1944/45–MAY 1945

Grenadiers from the 3rd Army quench their thirst before resuming their relentless struggle against Russian forces in February 1945. In February the 3rd Army was one of the armies that made up the new Army Group Vistula. On 10 March, General Hasso von Manteuffel was made the commander of the 3rd Army, which was assigned to defend the banks of the Oder River, north of the Seelow Heights, thus preventing the Soviets access to Western Pomerania and the Reich capital. (HITM)

A German soldier takes aim behind the cover of a railway embankment in Pomerania, late February 1945. The stiff German defence of Pomerania remained a thorn in the side of the Soviet army well into the spring of 1945. (Ullstein Bilderdienst)

Two Hummels halted on a road. The Hummel mounted a standard 15cm heavy field howitzer in a lightly-armoured fighting compartment built on the chassis of a PzKpfw IV. This heavy self-propelled gun carried just 18 15cm rounds, but was potent against Soviet armour. (HITM)

A variant of a Sturmpanzer Brummbär prior to its deployment to Hungary. This vehicle was probably attached to the Sturmpanzerabteilung 219. The Sturmpanzer unit was moved to Hungary in early 1945 and saw widespread action with the 23rd Panzer Division. (HITM)

PART III: WINTER 1944/45–MAY 1945

A MG42 machine gunner scours a lake near Stettin using a pair of 6x30 binoculars in late March 1945. It was on 30 March on the Oder front, that German troops finally evacuated their last remaining bridgehead at Wollin just north of Stettin, leaving the town to be captured by Russian forces. (HITM)

Three SdKfz 251 halftracks halted inside a village in eastern Germany bound for the front lines in late March 1945. Throughout the war the performance of the grenadiers and Panzergrenadiers in battle was attributed mainly to the halftrack, which transported these infantry units onto the battlefield. Even during the last desperate weeks of the war the halftrack was used as it had always been, to carry the infantry, to tow anti-tank and anti-aircraft guns, howitzers, and pontoon-bridge sections to the forefront of the battle. (HITM)

A dead soldier is draped over a 15cm Nebelwerfer 41. This deadly six-barrelled rocket launcher fired 2.5 kg shells that could be projected over a range of 7,000 metres. When fired the projectiles screamed through the air, causing the enemy to become unnerved by the noise. These fearsome weapons that caused extensive carnage to enemy positions served in independent army rocket launcher battalions, and later in the war in regiments and brigades. (HITM)

Troops pose onboard one of the last remaining Sturmpanzer Brummbär, which mounted the 15cm StuH 43 L/12 gun on the Panzer IV chassis. This vehicle belonged to the 23rd Panzer Division, which fought extensively during the last months of the war in Hungary, where it was almost completely destroyed. (HITM)

PART III: WINTER 1944/45–MAY 1945

A German soldier with a *Volksdeutsche* volunteer armed with Panzerfausts during the last months of the war in 1945. During urbanized fighting the Panzerfaust's short sight lines allowed the weapon to be easily used and this proved particularly deadly. Thousands of these disposable weapons were issued to the German Army, Volkssturm, Volksdeutsche volunteers and other various party forces. With these handheld rocket weapons large numbers of Soviet armoured vehicles were knocked out, especially during the battle of Berlin. The Panzerfaust was so easily constructed that they could be made in the city whilst under siege, allowing wheelbarrow loads of Panzerfausts to be delivered to the defenders. (HITM)

7. Last Battles around Berlin

In the last months of the war on the Eastern Front, German infantry divisions tried their best to form some kind of defensive line along an increasingly shrinking front. Exhausted and demoralised skeletal units that had been fighting for survival in previous weeks were now fully aware of the impending defeat in the East. Yet the German General Staff was still determined to fight at all costs, even if it meant throwing together unfit or badly depleted regiments and battalions.

In late March 1945, less than 100 miles east of Berlin, German infantry and Panzer troops were compelled to hold the front against superior Soviet artillery and aviation. In that sector, most of the front lay on the western bank of the Oder, but there were two major bridgeheads still on the eastern bank: in the north, the historic town of Stettin; to the south, the city of Frankfurt-an-der-Oder. Both sat directly opposite Berlin.

There were two armies holding the front to prevent the Russians from continuing their drive and capturing the German capital. On the northern wing was the 3rd Panzer Army under the command of General Hasso von Manteuffel. Eighty miles away in the south was General Theodor Busse and his 9th Army. The 9th Army had suffered immeasurably on the Eastern Front. From one collapsed sector to another, the force of some 250,000 soldiers had slowly withdrawn to the Oder. On its way, it cannibalised vehicles to keep it going and ruthlessly destroyed guns and equipment that could no longer be used.

Desperately short of combat-tested troops, most units in both the 3rd Panzer and 9th Army had been bolstered with remnants of once-proud divisions long since destroyed. With crippling shortages of every kind both armies fought out the last weeks of the war against an opponent some two million strong. Desperately they held their positions, but by the last week of March 1945, the city of Küstrin became encircled. In spite of every effort to relieve the city, German formations failed.

The 9th Army had suffered incredible losses trying to hold onto the city, but the Russian superiority was far too great and it fell into Red Army hands. The Russian onslaught did not end at Küstrin but was to be the springboard for the Soviet drive on Berlin. Within days, the men of the elite Russian 8th Guards Army launched a massive assault against the critical Seelow Heights, sacrificing literally thousands of men in the process. The 9th Army had taken the full brunt of the Russian attacks, and was slowly wilting under the constant hammer blows of enemy artillery. Yet Busse's forces were still holding in a number of places.

At Frankfurt-an-der-Oder, they had actually thrown the enemy back. Although mercilessly bombed and shelled at Seelow, the men doggedly and persistently pinned the enemy down. But their ardent defensive tactics had cost them dearly. In some areas, officers reported that they were outnumbered at least ten to one.

In the first weeks of April 1945, as the German Army waited for the final onslaught along the Oder, the atmosphere in all units became a mixture of terrible foreboding and despair. As for the Russian soldiers, the mood was tense but confident.

On 15 April 1945, Hitler sent an Order of the Day directly to Busse's 9th Army headquarters to appeal to his soldiers, who he regarded were the last bastion of defence on the Eastern Front, to stand fast and fight to the death. It read:

> Soldiers of the German Eastern Front for the last time the deadly Jewish enemy is going over to the attack with his hordes. He is trying to smash Germany and eliminate our people. You soldiers in the East already know the fait that threatens … German women, girls and children. The old men and children will be murdered; women and girls will be reduced to army camp whores. The remainder will go to Siberia. We have expected this attack, and since January everything has been done to build up a strong front. The enemy is confronted by a tremendous amount of artillery. Losses in our infantry have been filled with countless new units. Alarm units, newly organised units and the Volkssturm are reinforcing our front. This time the Bolshevist will experience the old fate of Asia: he must and shall fall before the capital city of the German Reich. Whoever does not do his duty at this moment is a traitor to our people. Any regiment or division that leaves its position acts so disgracefully that it must be ashamed before the women and children who are withstanding the bombing terror in our cities. Take heed specially of the few traitorous officers and soldiers who, in order to save their miserable lives, will fight against us for Russian pay, perhaps even wearing German Army uniforms. Anyone ordering you to retreat, unless you know him well, is to be taken prisoner at once and if necessary killed on the spot, no matter what his rank may be. If every soldier does his duty on the Eastern Front in the coming days and weeks, the last onrush from Asia will be broken, exactly as in the end the penetration of our enemy in the west will fail in spite of everything.

General Busse did not need any lengthy orders from his Führer to tell him that the Red Army had to be halted at all costs. But he was angry to read Hitler's talk of a strong front; of an enemy confronted by a strong line of artillery. In his view Hitler's urgent requests were pure 'fiction', and all he wanted from the German Army was for them to sacrifice themselves on the battlefield. Although Busse told Hitler that he would do what he could to stem the Russian onslaught bearing down on Berlin, the General was already hoping that if his forces could stand fast on the Oder long enough, then the Americans would arrive. He quietly voiced his thoughts to General Gotthard Heinrici:

> If we can hold until the Americans get here we will have fulfilled our mission before our people, our country and history. Germany's position is hopeless and so is that of the 9th Army. But as long as Hitler continues to fight the war he could only try and hold the Soviets up to the very last moment.

In front of Berlin, as the last battle was about to be waged in the East, company commanders of Army Group Vistula tried to persuade their soldiers to hold fast. The Oder Neisse fronts were about to be engulfed by the greatest concentration of firepower ever amassed. General Zhukov's 1st Belorussian Front and Konev's 1st Ukrainian Front were preparing to attack German forces defending positions east of Berlin. For the attack, the Soviets forces mustered over two million men and divided them into four powerful armies. They were supported by 41,600 guns and heavy mortars as well as 6,250 tanks and self-propelled guns.

The final battle before Berlin began at dawn on 16 April 1945. Just 38-miles east of the swollen River Oder, red flares burst into the night sky, triggering a massive artillery barrage. For nearly an hour, an eruption of flame and smoke burst along the German front. Then, in the mud, smoke and darkness General Zhukov's soldiers charged into action. As they surged forward, the artillery barrage remained in front of them, covering the area ahead. General Busse described the bombardment as the worst he had ever experienced. But despite the pulverising bombardment on its front lines, it seemed the bulk of Army Group Vistula had been saved from complete devastation.

Under the cover of darkness on the night of 15th, most of the German forward units had been moved back to a second line just before the expected Russian artillery barrage. In this second line, as the first rays of light prevailed along the Oder, soldiers waited for the advancing Russians. Along the entire front dispersed among the 3rd and 9th armies they had fewer than 700 tanks and self-propelled guns. The strongest division, the 25th Panzer, had just 79 such vehicles; the smallest unit had just two. Artillery too was equally poor with only 744 guns. Ammunition and fuel were in a critical state of supply and reserves in some units were non-existent. Opposing the main Russian assault on the crucial Seelow Heights stood the LVI Panzer Corps. It was under the command of General Karl Weidling, known to his friends as 'smasher Karl'. Weidling had been given the awesome task of preventing the main Russian breakthrough in the area.

At dawn as the Red Army advanced hundreds of German flak guns that had been hastily transferred from the Western Front to the East, poured a hurricane of fire into the Red Army troops. All morning, shells and gunfire rained down on the Russians, blunting their attack. By early evening the Russians were forced to withdraw and by the following morning, 17 April, they still had not breached the strong German defences. But General Zhukov was determined to batter the enemy into submission and ruthlessly bulldoze his way through to Berlin. By the mid-afternoon, with total disregard of casualties, Russian troops began smashing through the German defences. Soon confusion swept the decimated German lines. Soldiers who had fought doggedly from one fixed position to another were seized with panic. With the 9th Army constantly sustaining a hurricane of fire, the Seelow Heights finally fell to the Red Army. The town of Seelow itself was then attacked on 18 April, and taken street by street.

In three days of fighting, thousands of German soldiers had perished. Despite their attempt to blunt the Red Army, the road to Berlin was finally wrenched open. Bewildered German commanders struggled desperately to hold their forces together. Those German forces that had not been swallowed up and destroyed by the Russians withdrew in confusion. By 21 April, the Red Army had finally broken through the German front line in two places and started to surround Berlin. The 9th Army was between the two massive Russian pincers that were heading for the capital. The southern pincer consisted of the 1st Ukrainian Front under the command of Ivan Konev. His army had successfully cut through the area behind the 9th Army front lines. Busse's command was facing catastrophe, yet the German General was not considering pulling back. With the army denied any freedom of movement, it was certain to be destroyed.

By 22 April, Busse's force was almost encircled and close to annihilation. In spite of orders from the Führer's headquarters in Berlin that the line of defence on the Oder must never be abandoned, the General, with the larger half of the 9th Army consisting of some 80,000 soldiers of the XI SS Panzer Corps, the V SS Gebirgsjäger Corps and the garrison of Frankfurt-an-der-Oder, began to withdraw south-westwards towards the Spreewald in an attempt to link up with the German armies' youngest commander, General Walther Wenck and his 12th Army. Within days, the 9th Army, still doggedly battling towards Wenck's forces, was totally surrounded and being continuously hammered night and day by Russian bombers. The supply situation was dire. The Luftwaffe attempted a number of airdrops, but everything went wrong. There were not enough aircraft, and the planes that were used dropped in the wrong places.

The entire northern flank of 9th Army then collapsed. The remnants of the army shuffled along roads, tracks and fields trying to escape the slaughter. Vehicles were abandoned as they ran out of fuel along the way. During their tortuous journey, the exhausted troops moved into a forest near the large village of Halbe. It was here that remnants of 9th Army would endure what most of the survivors called the 'slaughter at Halbe'.

It was here in the Halbe forest that some 80,000 troops from Busse's 9th Army had withdrawn in a desperate attempt to link up with General Wenck's 12th Army. As the 9th Army withdrew, the troops of the 1st Belorussian Front and the 1st Ukrainian Front followed in their wake leaving a trail of devastation. Panic and disorganisation seemed to characterise Busse's withdrawal as his forces were compressed into a pocket in the forest. Over the next few days the conditions in which the Germans continued to fight were horrific. Cut off and facing almost total annihilation Busse was determined to break through the encirclement and reach the west. Any thoughts of pushing forward with Wenck's forces to relieve Berlin were totally out of the question. Instead, Busse refused to acknowledge the frantic appeals from the Führer headquarters and began planning a mass breakout in order to link up with Wenck's forces.

By 29 April some 25,000 troops succeeded in getting through the Russian lines and reaching Wenck's army around the town of Beelitz. Although the breakout was considered a success, more than 55,000 German troops were captured or killed in just over a week of fighting.

PART III: WINTER 1944/45–MAY 1945

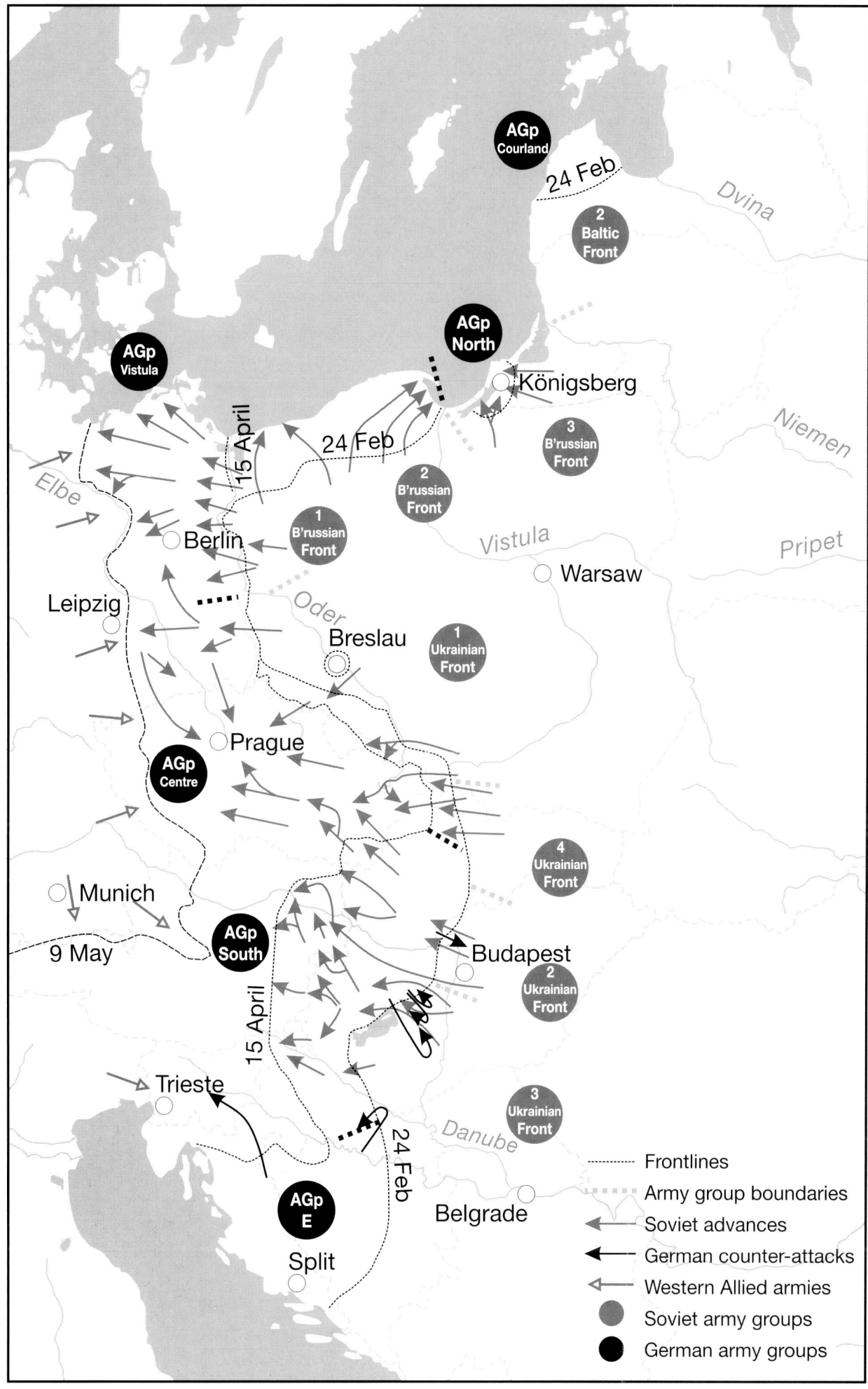

Map 5: Eastern Front, Berlin offensive and final Soviet operations 1944-45

FROM RETREAT TO DEFEAT

The crew of a 2cm Flak gun prepare their weapon for action along the Vistula Front in early 1945. The guns assigned to a typical light Flak battery varied over time. Initially there were twelve 2cm and/or 3.7cm guns in four platoons of three. By 1945 this strength had been far reduced to less than a quarter in a Flak battery. (HITM)

The same flak crew photographed in sequence shows the gunner seated and elevating 2cm barrel skyward with the use of the gun elevation wheel. The flak gun has a number of barrel kill rings painted in white on the gun barrel. This type of practice was widespread in German military units and it indicated how many enemy targets the weapon had destroyed. Some guns saw a great deal of service and scored so many hits that it was difficult to accurately count them. Note in the distance a well dug-in 8.8cm Flak gun with winter whitewash paint. (HITM)

The last photograph in the same sequence showing the flak gun. The gunner can clearly be seen looking through the gun's flak sight, which was a reflecting mirror sight that could calculate course and speed. Although the light anti-aircraft gun was used extensively to deal with the unceasing threat of the Soviet Air Force, the masses of Russian armour compelled many flak crews to divert their attention from the air and support their own infantry and armour on the ground in an anti-tank or anti-personnel role. (HITM)

A MG42 machine squad during a brief respite on the Vistula Front in February 1945. With the deteriorating situation in Poland German forces between the Oder and Vistula Rivers were amalgamated into a new Army group named 'Army Group Vistula'. The creation of the new Army Group came about due to growing signs that the Red Army offensive was losing impetus. Russian forward units had run short of supplies, fuel and ammunition allowing some valuable time for the German Army to hastily put together the new Army Group. (HITM)

PART III: WINTER 1944/45–MAY 1945

A well dug in battery of flak guns in action against enemy targets in Army Group Vistula in February 1945. During the later half of the war, as heavier and more lethal Soviet armour was brought to bear against the German Army, German forces clamoured to obtain more flak guns that could deal with the increasing enemy threat. By 1945, all of the flak guns were assigned in dual-purpose roles in order to try and stem the overwhelming steel tracks of the T-34 tank. (HITM)

Youthful German soldiers cycle through a Silesian village, late March 1945. The last months of the war in the East witnessed a number of German formations using bicycles to overcome transport difficulties. Such formations were often equipped with large numbers of Panzerfäuste, and sometimes given exotic names such as *Panzerjagdkommandos*. (Ullstein Bilderdienst)

113

German troops in Army Group Vistula are using a captured Russian artillery piece to help bolster their meagre positions along the Oder in February 1945. The gun is a Soviet M1942 ZIS-3 76mm gun. The Russians used this artillery piece extensively, the gun firing a range of high explosive and armour piecing ammunition. (HITM)

Grenadiers defending the Oder front in March 1945 armed with the lethal Panzerfaust. A Russian T-34 tank can be seen burning on the road following a Panzerfaust attack. The Panzerfaust was a series of handheld rocket-propelled grenades, which were effective at a range of about 90 feet. The Panzerfaust consisted of a hollow steel firing tube with the warhead projecting from the top end of it. The weapon was a single-shot piece. Once used, the hollow firing tube was discarded. (HITM)

PART III: WINTER 1944/45–MAY 1945

Grenadiers on the western bank of the Oder in March 1945. The soldier on the left is using a Czech-made ZB vz/30 machine gun, a second-rate weapon that saw service with a variety of miscellaneous German formations up until the end of the war. Most of the front was held on the western bank of the Oder, less than 100 miles from Berlin. The German Army tried their best to form some kind of defensive position along the Oder, in spite of the badly depleted odd regiments and battalions that were thrown in to help strengthen the lines. (HITM)

Grenadiers can be seen in one of the many trenches that composed the Oder Front. The core of the defence along the Oder rested on some 850 tanks and assault guns that had been collected from various units, reinforced by over 500 flak guns from Berlin's air-defence batteries. In total there were a series of six defensive lines that had been dug between the Oder and Berlin, directed by General Gotthard Heinrici, the new commander of the Oder Front. (HITM)

FROM RETREAT TO DEFEAT

Despite the catastrophic situation they found themselves in, morale remained high amongst many German units. Well-equipped German infantry prepare to move to the front, Pomerania, February 1945. The markings on the soldier's Panzerfaust are clearly visible – in particular, they warned the user to stay well clear of the backblast from the weapons tube when firing, the flames from which could easily sever an arm, or kill. (Ullstein Bilderdienst)

PART III: WINTER 1944/45–MAY 1945

Grenadiers, not far from the city of Küstrin, move forward to help reinforce troops of the 9th Army along the Oder in late March 1945. By the last week of March Küstrin was encircled. In spite of every effort to relieve the city, German formations failed. As a result, the 9th Army suffered high casualties trying to hold the city, but Russian superiority was far too great. (HITM)

A grenadier holding an ammunition case and a bolt-action rifle runs through a slit trench to quickly supply his number one with additional ammunition for his MG34 machine gun. In defence the machine guns were normally set up in forward platoon positions or were employed to overlook positions to the rear to provide long-range fire support, which included firing over the heads of friendly troops. (HITM)

Grenadiers rest in some undergrowth during the last weeks of the war. The men are armed with stick grenades and bolt action rifles. On their belts are ammunition pouches for the karabiner 98 K rifle. (HITM)

Grenadiers pose for the camera standing next to a goods train. Supplying front line troops on the Eastern Front had almost ceased to exist by April 1945. Not only were there limited stocks to be distributed to the German Army by this time, but also much of the railway system had been severely paralysed by heavy aerial bombing. (HITM)

PART III: WINTER 1944/45–MAY 1945

8. Berlin Falls

By mid-April 1945 it was fast becoming clear to all Berliners that for the first time their city was seriously under threat of a major siege. Inside the ruined city of Berlin thousands of civilians were frantically digging trenches and anti-tank obstacles on the eastern outskirts of the Reich capital. General Hellmuth Reymann, commander of 'Fortress Berlin', had been working around the clock for weeks trying feverishly to turn the city into a fortification. However, there were almost no mines available that were essential to a defensive position. Even barbed wire had become almost impossible to obtain. Reymann's artillery consisted of some mobile flak guns, several tanks dug in up to the turrets so that their guns covered approach roads, and the massive flak tower guns. Although they were powerful, they could not be deflected towards the ground to stave off close-range infantry and tank assaults. All over the smouldering city there were roadblocks and crude defence barriers, but Reymann was quite aware that 'Fortress Berlin' was far from completed. Even under ideal conditions, he believed, 200,000 fully trained and combat-seasoned soldiers would have been needed to defend the city. In stead, he had to hold Berlin's 600 square-miles with a range of motley assorted German Army and Waffen-SS groups that had been thrown together from various divisions that had been decimated on both the Eastern and Western Fronts. Among these groups were Hitlerjugend and 60,000 Volkssturm troops. These old men of the Volkssturm would have to bear the burden of defending the city defences. Although the Volkssturm were expected to fight alongside the German Army, they were not considered part of the army.

For all the troops that were pressed into defending Berlin they were subjected to merciless bombardments. In front of the city hard-pressed German troops were desperately trying to hold their slender positions, but the pulverising effects of Russian artillery had ground a depleted and exhausted force of men into a disjointed and discouraged one. Signs of disintegration plagued every sector of the front and the military situation was almost impossible to control. Desperate orders continued to emanate from the Headquarters in the Reich Chancellery Führer bunker as the remains of both the Reich and its capital were smashed to pieces by the invaders. But the troops defending the city were overwhelmed by the Red Army. As a consequence, district after district fell and the city's defence forces were beaten back. General Weidling, who was appointed the new commander of Berlin, did what he could by distributing the few remaining veterans of his battered LVI Panzer Corps to bolster the Volkssturm and Hitlerjugend. But still this did not alleviate the diminishing problem. To make matters worse news had reached the various command centres inside the city that General Busse's 9th Army had been encircled and unable to break through and help relieve Berlin.

By 29 April the Russians closed in on the centre of the city. In a desperate attempt to keep open a narrow route from the closing jaws of the enemy, Weidling mustered a few remaining veterans. For a number of hours German soldiers were engaged in a series of bitter and often bloody battles, trying with varying degrees of bravery to repulse the Red Army. But as the Russians isolated the city centre, Weidling was compressed more and more. The relief of Berlin now rested upon General Wenck's 12th Army. To the remaining soldiers that fought on inside the ravaged capital Wenck had become there only hope. But over the last few days remnants of the once vaunted troops from both Busse's 9th and Wenck's 12th Armies were not attempting to break through the Russian encirclement around Berlin. Instead they shuffled westwards towards American lines. Manteuffel's 3rd Panzer Army had also abandoned its fixed positions and were making a fighting withdrawal to the west. It too was escaping from the Russian, and its goal was surrendering to the Anglo-Americans. Berlin it seemed had been deserted by its army, and left to the Russians to conquer.

Inside the capital Weidling's communication networks no longer existed. Orders were now issued by word of mouth. The chaos was so bad that officers arriving to take over units discovered nothing to take over, because their commands had already been captured or annihilated. In most areas, inexperienced men like the Volkssturm were left leaderless and did not know exactly where they were fighting or who was fighting on their flanks. By the morning of 30 April virtually every German unit in Berlin were trapped, captured, overrun, or simply destroyed. Others that were demoralized just simply broke and ran. The remaining few troops that stood resolute against the Russians were now steadily driven back towards the governmental quarters of the city. Already Hitler's once great Reich Chancellery was under direct bombardment and one advance Russian unit was reported to have already advanced along the Wilhelmstrasse as far as the Air Ministry. But the key Russian objective was not the Reich Chancellery, but Berlin's most spectacular ruin, the huge Reichstag, seat of parliament before it was set ablaze in 1933. The Russians considered it the symbolic equivalent of their own Kremlin Moscow and were determined at all costs to capture it. For a number of hours the building was brought under heavy sustained fire by eighty-nine heavy Russian guns, but the German garrison was still intact, fighting fanatically. Through its crumbing six-columned entrance Russian troops stormed the building and began to fight. By the early afternoon of the thirtieth, the Soviet Red victory banner was hoisted above the Reichstag's dome.

FROM RETREAT TO DEFEAT

The battle for Berlin was effectively over, but fighting in the city continued for another twenty-four hours. Just after midnight on 2 May the Russian 79th Guards Rifle Division picked up a faint crackling radio message. 'Hello, hello', said the faint voice. 'This is the LVI Panzer Corps. We ask for a cease-fire'. On receipt of the message, General Chuikov ordered an immediate cease-fire. Just before one o'clock in the morning on 2 May, Weidling's Chief of Staff, Colonel von Dufving, and two other officers arrived at the Potsdam Bridge under the white flag. They were then escorted to Chuikov headquarters. Soon afterwards Weidling followed. Later that day powerful loud speakers all over bomb-battered Berlin announced the end of hostilities. Although for a few days sporadic fighting continued in some isolated areas, the battle for Berlin was officially over. Throughout the city Berliner's began rousing themselves from weeks they had spent in the cellars, subway stations, and bunkers. They had hidden under the reassurance of the Swastika. When they ventured out across the charred remains of their fallen city that afternoon the only flags they saw flying bore the hammer and sickle.

A MG34 machine gun squad cross a stretch of flooded water in a rubber inflatable boat. German army engineers had turned the Oder's flood plain, already partially flooded by water by the spring thaw, into a swamp by releasing the waters in a reservoir upstream. Behind this they built three belts of defensive emplacements, which reached back towards the outskirts of Berlin. General Heinrici, who was commander of Army Group Vistula, was one of the best defensive tacticians in the German Army and was determined to delay the Russians at whatever cost. (HITM)

Flak troops are attempting to dismount a well-camouflaged 8.8cm flak gun from the gun's limber. After the gun was positioned into place the gun's limber was placed nearby, and this was undertaken especially if employed in an anti-tank role where it was necessary to rapidly limber-up and re-position the gun. (HITM)

A MG34 machine gunner with ammunition feeder along dug-in positions during the battle of the Oder during April 1945. On the Oder front Army Group Vistula consisted of the 3rd and 9th Armies. Between both armies there were some 480,000 troops, but almost no reserves. Apart from the acute shortages of combat-tested troops, both armies were handicapped by massive shortages of equipment and supplies. (HITM)

A knocked out Hummel with its 15cm gun barrel half blown off is being examined by two soldiers. In total some 666 of these vehicles were built during the war until the programme was finally terminated in 1944. However, a number of them were still seen in active service in 1945, and soldiers witnessed a few fighting in the defence along the Oder. (HITM)

PART III: WINTER 1944/45–MAY 1945

A MG34 machine gun team from Busse's 9th Army take cover in some undergrowth as the battle for the Oder continues. On 16 April 1945 the Red Army launched the last great offensive against Hitler's Third Reich. By the next day the Red Army had still not breached the strong German defences. Although German troops had fought doggedly from one fixed position to another, the situation was bordering on the catastrophic. Bewildered German commanders still struggled desperately to hold their forces together. (HITM)

The charred and twisted remains of a number of vehicles are strewn in front of a bombed out church in April 1945. Two badly fire damaged Wespes can be seen. The aerial bombing campaign both on the Eastern and Western Fronts caused severe problems for the Panzerwaffe. During the last year of the war the bombing campaign had become so bad that many armoured crews could only move by night to avoid being attacked. (HITM)

It was not only around Berlin that Germans forces continued to resist during April and May 1945. This photograph shows the commander of a combat engineer company giving orders to his men, Moravia, April 1945. (Ullstein Bilderdienst)

PART III: WINTER 1944/45–MAY 1945

Troops pose for the camera in front of a 'Mule', better known as a Maultier. The Maultier was armed with a ten-tube 15cm Nebelwerfer 42 on the rear of a halftrack. A battery of these formidable weapons fought on the Oder Front in a vain effort to prevent the Red Army consolidating their bridgeheads on the west bank of the Oder. However, once the battery had expended all its munitions, it was quickly dissolved, for there were no more supplies readily available. (HITM)

Assault gun troops belonging to the decimated 9th Army in the Beelitz area in April 1945. A well-camouflaged StuG III Ausf.G can just be seen hidden between the trees. By 29 April some 25,000 exhausted German troops from the 9th Army with a handful of armoured vehicles had succeeded in escaping through the Russian lines and reaching the 12th Army around the town of Beelitz. (HITM)

A column of dejected Hungarian PoWs are escorted by Russian troops past a destroyed Jagdpanzer IV/70 in Budapest, early 1945. The Jagdpanzer was a well-liked and effective tank destroyer, which had knocked out many Russian tanks. However, like many of the later built armoured vehicles there were too few many to decisively change the conduct of operations on the battlefield. (HITM)

A later image from the same sequence showing Russian soldiers with Hungarian PoWs being led past the disabled Jagdpanzer IV/70. Although the Jagdpanzer an effective anti-tank capability by the time these vehicles appeared on the battlefield combat was defensive and their attributes on the Eastern Front little mattered any more. (HITM)

PART III: WINTER 1944/45–MAY 1945

Remains of two StuG IIIs destroyed and abandoned in a lake somewhere in eastern Germany in 1945. The StuG had done sterling service on the Eastern Front, but after all the reserves had gone the Panzerwaffe was only a shadow of its former self. It continued to fight on against overwhelming odds until the last days of the war. (HITM)

German PoWs shuffle along a muddy road past an abandoned StuG III Ausf G in 1945. The German soldier had certainly done his duty to the last. Many units on the Eastern Front had sacrificed themselves in order to frantically hold their weakened lines and keep back the enemy for as along as possible. (HITM)

Elements of a signals unit belonging to Panzergrenadier Division 'Grossdeutschland' attempt to make contact with units of the German navy during the evacuation from Heiligenbeil, via the Frisches Haff to Hela, March 1945. (Ullstein Bilderdienst)

A StuG III Ausf G sits abandoned on a Berlin street after the fall of the Reich capital in May 1945. The war on the Eastern Front was finally over for the German Army. The fighting had lasted three years, ten months, and sixteen days and culminated with the complete devastation of Berlin. During this long battle in the East the casualties were immense. According to German records more than three million German soldiers had been killed; many of the losses were during the last years of the war. After the failure at Kursk, from which the German war effort was never to recover, the Germany Army found itself in retreat, losing massive amounts of men and equipment which it could not properly replace. For nearly two years, covering more than 1200 miles, the once-mighty German Army retreated across Russia leaving nothing but a burnt and devastated wasteland. At the gates of Berlin it fought out its last desperate battle until it finally surrendered to a victorious Red Army. (HITM)

PART III: WINTER 1944/45–MAY 1945

Two photographs taken of the same StuG III Ausf G. The assault vehicle has been knocked out and lies abandoned in a rubble-strewn street in eastern Germany in 1945. The StuG III was not a very effective armoured vehicle for urbanized fighting owing to its fixed gun. However, its lethal 7.5cm barrel gave the assault gun added punch against enemy vehicles and various defensive positions. Troops too used the StuG for infantry support, in spite of its increased anti-tank role during the later part of the war. (HITM)

Epilogue

Following the surrender of Berlin on 2 May 1945, the will to fight of the remaining forces still attempting to defend parts of eastern Germany, notably the scattered remnants of what was left of Army Group Vistula, quickly came to an end. In Schwerin the American 9th Army pushed east and captured the Army Group Vistula headquarters. The Russian 2nd Belorussian Front reached Wittenberg, Parchim, and Bad Doberan. Between both the American and Russian fronts the remains of the once vaunted 3rd Panzer and 21st Armies were compressed into a corridor no more than twenty-miles wide, stretching from the coast to the river Elbe. During the night both armies, which had all but disintegrated, surrendered to the Americans.

Further south Wenck's 12th Army had begun to withdraw southwest of Potsdam and by the morning of 1 May it had taken some 30,000 survivors from Busse's 9th Army through its line. Miraculously remnants of both army groups had escaped the impending slaughter against the strongest of Russian concentrations around Berlin and had trudged westward with the sole intention of surrendering their exhausted and badly depleted forces to the US 9th Army. On the afternoon of 3 May Wenck sent General Maximillian Freiherr von Edelsheim across the Elbe to negotiate surrender with the US 9th Army. The following morning it was agreed that troops of both the 9th and 12th Armies could cross the Elbe with the exception of casualties and take refuge behind American lines.

Whilst Wenck and Busse's forces withdrew across the Elbe into American captivity, Army Groups Centre, Kurland and East Prussia, the last bastions of defence on the Eastern Front, were ordered by Admiral Doenitz to start retreating westward at once. Almost 150,000 troops from Army Group Centre and Army Group East Prussia moved westwards and surrendered to American and British forces.

APPENDIX I

German Army Uniforms

The main service uniform worn in the German Army throughout the war on the Eastern Front was the Model 1936 or M36 regular army service uniform. This popular garment was field-grey in colour and manufactured from wool/rayon mixed material. It had four box-pleated pockets with a single metal finish button sewn to each of the four three pocket flaps. There were also five metal buttons sewn down the front of the tunic. The collar of the tunic was faced with dark blue-green material and sewn into this was the German Army collar patch indicating NCOs and other ranks. The shoulder straps made from dark blue-green material were sewn into the shoulders of the tunic at the arm end and positioned at the other with a single metal button. The shoulder strap could also be used to hold the soldier's military equipment in place on the shoulders.

Stitched on the right of the tunic above the breast pocket was the national emblem of Germany. This silver emblem consisted of an eagle with outstretched wings clutching in its talons a wreath containing a swastika. Another item of cloth normally sewn onto the uniform was the German Army rank chevron and occasionally the specialist insignia, trade and specialist badge. All types of arm rank chevrons and specialist badges were worn on the upper left arm of the uniform tunic, the service and field service tunics as well as the greatcoats.

Worn around the tunic waist was the army service brown leather belt with silver metal or aluminium buckle. When the soldier had his personal equipment the wearer's leather support straps, ammunition pouches, and other important field equipment needed to sustain him on the battlefield were attached to the main tunic belt.

Apart from the tunic, the other item of clothing worn to accompany the service uniform was the trousers. These were normally field-grey in colour and were high-waisted with a top button. The trousers had four fly buttons, two of which were stitched at a slanted angle and designed either with pocket flaps or no flaps at all, depending on the manufacturer.

Footwear for the service uniform usually consisted of black leather marching boots, leather-riding boots with adjustable straps and short lace-up ankle boots used mainly by the *Gebirgsjäger*.

By 1943 a new model service tunic was issued to the troops in Russia called the Model 1943 or M43. The design of the M43 uniform no longer had box-pleated pockets, nor did it have dark blue-green collar material. Instead it was made in field-grey cloth. Generally though the uniform was very similar to that of the M36, but the quality was poorer. Wearers also complained that the tunic was not well insulated and became very heavy when subjected to sustained downpours of rain.

In spite of the shoddy appearance of the new M43 service uniform, it was generally hard-wearing and was worn by thousands of soldiers during this period of the war. However, by 1944 with the German Army still embroiled in bitter conflict a completely revised style of field service uniform was rushed into production, called the Model 1944 or M44.

The M44 service uniform was radically different from the traditional German Army uniform worn, and designers had actually adopted the style very similar to that of the British Army uniform blouse. The colour of the uniform was grey-green. The jacket had two large pockets without pleats but with pocket flaps, which was fastened by a single metal button. The German national emblem was still worn on the right breast above the pocket. There were shoulder straps displaying the wearer's rank and the cuffs to the sleeves were designed very similar to that of the standard German army service tunic. The collar was of the same material as the blouse and was in the late pattern mouse-grey colour.

The M44 became a very popular service uniform during the last year of the war and was worn by both the German Army and the *Waffen-SS* in Russia and other theatres of war.

One of the last items of clothing to be worn by the German Army in Russia, which was regarded as a service uniform, was the reed-green denim field service uniform. This was introduced in the summer of 1944 and was a very successful and popular uniform worn by soldiers on the front lines. Both the jacket and the trousers were lightweight and hard wearing and were of matching reed green herringbone pattern denim. The garment carried the normal insignia. The trousers to the uniform were in the normal field-grey colour and were in the same style and quality to that of the jacket.

Another popular item of clothing worn by the German Army on the Eastern Front during the harsh winters was the reversible winter uniform. The troops were issued with these garments in October and November 1942. They found the clothing extremely warm and comfortable. The uniform also provided the wearer with greater freedom of movement, especially with personal equipment. This uniform not only helped combat the severity of the cold, but helped prevent overheating during physical exertion.

The reversible clothing itself consisted of a heavy reversible double-breasted over-jacket that was designed for extra frontal warmth. The trousers worn were thick, as was the jacket, and were completely reversible. They were shorter in length to normal standard issue uniformed trousers but could be either worn over the top of the leather marching boots or tucked inside. The ends of the trousers were gathered in by drawstrings and tied in around the boots.

The winter reversible was normally mouse-grey on one side and winter white on the other. The soldiers wore the reversible garment depending on the terrain. If the area was snow-covered the wearer wore the uniform on the winter white side out, and during operations where there was no snow, it was worn mouse-grey side out. However, there were other variations of the reversible, which included the green splinter pattern and the tan water pattern.

The reversible uniform was designed large enough to be worn over the service uniform, including personal equipment. However, troops did favour wearing most of their equipment over the winter jacket.

During the last two years of the war the German soldier was seen wearing these popular winter camouflage garments, together with a number of older style winter camouflage smocks. By the winter of 1943, the winter reversible had become one of the most popular items of winter clothing worn by the troops. As a result of these warm insulated camouflaged items of clothing soldier survivability had actually increased, in spite of the major military setbacks.

APPENDIX II

Personal Equipment and Weapons

The German soldier was very well equipped, perhaps the best in the world in 1939. The rifleman or *Schütze* wore the trademark model 1935/1942 steel helmet, which provided ample protection whilst marching to the battlefront and during combat. His leather belt with support straps carried two sets of three ammunition pouches for a total of 60 rounds for his carbine. The soldier also wore his combat harness for his mess kit and special camouflage rain cape or *Zeltbahn*. He also wore an entrenching tool, and attached to the entrenching tool carrier was the bayonet, a bread bag for rations, gas mask canister, which was invariably slung over the wearer's shoulder and an anti-gas cape in its pouch attached to the shoulder strap. The infantryman's flashlight was normally attached to the tunic and inside the tunic pocket he carried wound dressings. A small backpack was issued to the soldiers, though some did not wear them. The backpack was intended for spare clothing, personal items, and additional rations along with a spare clothing satchel.

The weapons used by the German soldier varied, but the standard issue piece of equipment was the 7.92mm Kar98k carbine, even by 1943. This excellent modern and effective bolt-action rifle was of Mauser design. This rifle remained the most popular weapon used by the German Army throughout the war. Another weapon used by the German Army, but not to the extent used by the Kar98k, was the 9mm MP38 or MP40 machine pistol. This submachine gun was undoubtedly one of the most effective weapons ever produced for the German war machine. Other weapons included the revolutionary MP 43 machine pistol. This gun could also fire standard rifle/machine gun rounds of 7.92mm calibre but filled with a lower charge to reduce recoil. Anther German infantry weapon used during the last two years of the war was the Sturmgewehr 44. This weapon was intended to be the main short-range machine pistol of the German Army, but due to economical conditions imposed on the German armament industry, too few were issued to be an effective replacement. One of the most effective and successful weapons to be issued to the German Army was the 7.92mm MG34 light machine gun. This was yet another weapon that featured heavily within the ranks of the German Army. The effectiveness of the weapon made it the most superior machine gun ever produced at that time. The MG34 and the MG42 possessed a very impressive fire rate and could dominate the battlefield both in defensive and offensive roles. The German Army possessed the MG34 in every rifle group, and machine gun crews were able to transport this relatively light weapon easily onto the battlefield by resting it over the shoulder.

Other weapons, which were seen at both company and battalion level on the battlefield, were the 5cm lGrW36 light mortar and 8cm sGrW34 heavy mortar. Although they could both be an effective weapon when fired accurately the light and heavy mortar was far too heavy and too expensive to produce on a very large scale. One piece of weaponry that was light but inexpensive to produce on a large scale were rocket propelled weapons. With the dramatic change in German tactics on the battlefield, especially when fighting against masses of Russian armour, the Germans designed rocket-propelled grenades that could be fired either by one soldier or a team of two. These effective weapons were short-range, which meant that German soldiers were compelled to fight at close quarters against enemy armour. The first of these weapons to be massed produced and issued to the German Army was the Panzerfaust 30 or Faustpatrone 2. This weapon could launch rocket-propelled grenades at a range of 30 metres, at that distance the grenade could penetrate 18cm of armour. The Panzerfaust 30 was a very light mobile weapon that could be fired from a variety of positions, including kneeling, standing and resting on the firer's shoulder or across his right arm. The only drawback was, like all Panzerfaust weapons, this was a single-shot piece. Once it was fired, the hollow firing tube was thrown away. During the last years of the war a number of Panzerfaust were issued to front line troops and these varied from the Panzerfaust 30 *Klein*, Panzerfaust 60, Panzerfaust 100, and the two-man anti-tank rocket weapon, the *Raketen Panzerbüchse* 5.

At regimental and divisional level the German Army possessed its own artillery in the form of the 10.5cm lFH18, 15cm sFH18, and 15cm sIG33 infantry guns. Specially-trained artillery crews used these popular guns and they were seen in action throughout the war. Another weapon that was used throughout the war was the 3.7cm Pak35/36. However, by 1943, it was in diminishing numbers as *Panzerjäger* crews had long become aware of the tactical limitations of the weapon, especially against heavy Russian armour. By this period of the war the German Army had already affirmed faith in its new generation anti-tank guns like the 5cm Pak 38, the deadly 7.5cm Pak 40 and the powerful 8.8cm Pak 43. The Pak 43 became the finest anti-tank gun to see operational service during the war on the Eastern Front. The weapon proved to be so lethal on the battlefield against enemy armour that it was soon recognised to be far superior to that of the dual-purpose 8.8cm Flak 41.

APPENDIX III

Organisation, unit listings

Infantry Divisions

Below is a complete list of infantry divisions, together with Volksgrenadier, Fortress, Reserve, Field Training, Static, Motorized and and Luftwaffe formations.

1st Infantry Division
3rd Motorized Infantry Division (later 3rd Panzergrenadier Division)
4th Infantry Division (later 14th Panzer Division)
5th Infantry Division (later 5th Light Infantry Division, 5th Jäger Division)
6th Infantry Division (later 6th Grenadier Division, 6th Volksgrenadier Division)
7th Infantry Division
8th Infantry Division (later 8th Light Infantry Division, 8th Jäger Division)
9th Infantry Division (later 9th Volksgrenadier Division)
10th Infantry Division (later 10th Motorized Infantry Division, 10th Panzergrenadier Division)
11th Infantry Division
12th Infantry Division (later 12th Volksgrenadier Division)
14th Infantry Division (later 14th Motorized Infantry Division, then 14th Infantry Division again)
14th Luftwaffe Field Division
15th Infantry Division
15th Panzergrenadier Division (previously 33rd Infantry Division, 15th Panzer Division)
16th Infantry Division
16th Motorized Infantry Division (later 16th Panzergrenadier Division, 116th Panzer Division)
16th Luftwaffe Field Division (later 16th Volksgrenadier Division)
17th Infantry Division
18th Infantry Division (later 18th Motorised Infantry Division, 18th Panzergrenadier Division)
18th Volksgrenadier Division
19th Infantry Division (later 19th Panzer Division)
19th Grenadier Division (later 19th Volksgrenadier Division)
20th Motorized Infantry Division (later 20th Panzergrenadier Division)
21st Infantry Division
22nd Infantry Division (later 22nd Air Landing Division, 22nd Volksgrenadier Division)
23rd Infantry Division (later 26th Panzer Division)
24th Infantry Division
25th Infantry Division (later 25th Motorized Infantry Division)
25th Panzergrenadier Division
26th Infantry Division (later 26th Volksgrenadier Division)
27th Infantry Division (later 17th Panzer Division)
28th Light Infantry Division (later 28th Jäger Division)
29th Motorized Infantry Division (later 29th Panzergrenadier Division)
30th Infantry Division
31st Infantry Division (later 31st Grenadier Division, 31st Volksgrenadier Division)
32nd Infantry Division
33rd Infantry Division (later 15th Panzer Division, 15th Panzergrenadier Division)
34th Infantry Division
35th Infantry Division (later 35th Volksgrenadier Division)
36th Infantry Division (later 36th Motorized Infantry Division, then 36th Infantry Division again, 36th Grenadier Division, and finally 36th Volksgrenadier Division)
38th Infantry Division
39th Infantry Division (later 41st Fortress Division, 41st Infantry Division)
41st Infantry Division (previously 39th Infantry Division, 41st Fortress Division)
42nd Jäger Division (previously 187th Reserve Division)
44th Infantry Division (later 44th Reichsgrenadier Division 'Hoch und Deutschmeister')
45th Infantry Division (later 45th Grenadier Division, 45th Volksgrenadier Division)
46th Infantry Division
47th Infantry Division (previously Division Nr. 156, 156th Reserve Division; later 47th Volksgrenadier Division)
48th Infantry Division (later 48th Volksgrenadier Division)

49th Infantry Division
50th Infantry Division
52nd Infantry Division (later 52nd Field Training Division, 52nd Security Division)
56th Infantry Division
57th Infantry Division
58th Infantry Division
59th Infantry Division
60th Infantry Division
61st Infantry Division (later 61st Volksgrenadier Division)
62nd Infantry Division (later 62nd Volksgrenadier Division)
64th Infantry Division
65th Infantry Division
68th Infantry Division
69th Infantry Division
70th Static Infantry Division
71st Infantry Division
72nd Infantry Division
73rd Infantry Division
75th Infantry Division
76th Infantry Division
77th Infantry Division
78th Infantry Division (later 78th Sturm Division, 78th Grenadier Division, 78 Volksgrenadier Division, and finally 78 Volks-Sturm Division)
79th Infantry Division (later 79th Volksgrenadier Division)
80th Infantry Division
81st Infantry Division
82nd Infantry Division
83rd Infantry Division
84th Infantry Division
85th Infantry Division
86th Infantry Division
87th Infantry Division
88th Infantry Division
89th Infantry Division
90th Light Infantry Division (previously the Division zbV Afrika; later 90th Light Afrika Division, 90th Panzergrenadier Division)
91st Infantry Division (later 91st Air Landing Division)
92nd Infantry Division
93rd Infantry Division
94th Infantry Division
95th Infantry Division (later 95th Volksgrenadier Division)
96th Infantry Division
97th Light Infantry Division (later 97th Jäger Division)
98th Infantry Division
99th Light Infantry Division (later 7th Mountain Division)
100th Light Infantry Division (later 100th Jäger Division)
101st Light Infantry Division (later 101st Jäger Division)
102nd Infantry Division
104th Jäger Division
106th Infantry Division
110th Infantry Division
114th Jäger Division
117th Jäger Division
118th Jäger Division
133rd Fortress Division
Division zbV 140 (also 9th Mountain Division)
141st Reserve Division
143rd Reserve Division
147th Reserve Division
148th Reserve Division
149th Field Training Division
150th Field Training Division
Division Nr. 151 (later 151st Reserve Division)
Division Nr. 152
Division Nr. 153 (later 153rd Reserve Division, 153rd Field Training Division, 153rd Grenadier Division)
Division Nr. 154 (later 154th Reserve Division, 154th Field Training Division, 154th Infantry Division)
Division Nr. 155 (later Division Nr. 155 (mot.), Panzer Division Nr. 155, 155th Reserve Panzer Division)
155th Field Training Division (later 155th Infantry Division)
Division Nr. 156 (later 156th Reserve Division, 47th Infantry Division, 47th Volksgrenadier Division)
156th Field Replacement Division (later 156th Infantry Division)
Division Nr. 157 (later 157th Reserve Division, 157th Mountain Division, 8th Mountain Division)
Division Nr. 158 (later 158th Reserve Division)
Division Nr. 159 (later 159th Reserve Division, 159th Infantry Division)
Division Nr. 160 (later 160th Reserve Division, 160th Infantry Division)
162nd Infantry Division (later 162nd Infantry Division Turkestan, with foreign troops)
163rd Infantry Division
164th Infantry Division (later Fortress Division Kreta, which split into 164th Light Afrika Division)
165th Reserve Division
166th Reserve Division
167th Volksgrenadier Division
169th Infantry Division
170th Infantry Division
171st Reserve Division
172nd Reserve Division
173rd Reserve Division
174th Reserve Division
181st Infantry Division
182nd Reserve Division

APPENDIX III: ORGANISATION, UNIT LISTINGS

- 183rd Volksgrenadier Division
- 187th Reserve Division (later 42nd Jäger Division)
- Division Nr. 188 (later 188th Reserve Mountain Division, 188th Mountain Division)
- 189th Reserve Division
- 191st Reserve Division
- 196th Infantry Division
- 198th Infantry Division
- 199th Infantry Division
- 201st Security Division
- 203rd Security Division
- 205th Infantry Division (previously 14th Landwehr Division)
- 206th Infantry Division
- 207th Infantry Division (later 207th Security Division)
- 208th Infantry Division
- 210th Coastal Defense Division
- 211th Volksgrenadier Division
- 212th Infantry Division (later later 578th Volksgrenadier Division, 212th Volksgrenadier Division)
- 213th Security Division
- 214th Infantry Division
- 217th Infantry Division
- 218th Infantry Division
- 221st Security Division
- 228th Infantry Division
- 230th Coastal Defense Division
- 233rd Panzergrenadier Division
- 242nd Static Infantry Division
- 243rd Static Infantry Division
- 246th Volksgrenadier Division
- 250th Infantry Division (División Azul, the Spanish 'Blue' Division in German service)
- 256th Infantry Division (Later 256th Volksgrenadier Division
- 257th Volksgrenadier Division
- 269th Infantry Division
- 270th Fortress Infantry Division
- 271st Volksgrenadier Division
- 272nd Volksgrenadier Division
- 274th Static Infantry Division
- 275th Infantry Division
- 276th Volksgrenadier Division
- 277th Volksgrenadier Division
- 280th Fortress Infantry Division
- 281st Security Division (later 281st Infantry Division)
- 285th Security Division
- 286th Security Division
- 291st Infantry Division
- 295th Infantry Division (later 295th Fortress Infantry Division)
- 302nd Static Infantry Division (later 302nd Infantry Division)
- 320th Volksgrenadier Division
- 325th Security Division
- 326th Volksgrenadier Division
- 331st Infantry Division
- 332nd Static Infantry Division (later 332nd Infantry Division)
- 334th Infantry Division
- 337th Volksgrenadier Division
- 340th Volksgrenadier Division
- 344th Static Infantry Division (later 344th Infantry Division)
- 345th Motorized Infantry Division
- 347th Volksgrenadier Division
- 349th Volksgrenadier Division
- 352nd Infantry Division (later 352nd Volksgrenadier Division)
- 361st Volksgrenadier Division
- 363rd Volksgrenadier Division
- 381st Field Training Division
- 382nd Field Training Division
- 386th Motorized Infantry Division
- 388th Field Training Division
- 390th Security Division
- 390th Field Training Division
- 391st Security Division
- 391st Field Training Division
- 402nd Training Division
- 403rd Security Division
- 444th Security Division
- 454th Security Division
- 462nd Volksgrenadier Division
- 526th Reserve Division
- 541st Grenadier Division (later 541st Volksgrenadier Division)
- 542nd Grenadier Division (later 542nd Volksgrenadier Division)
- 543rd Grenadier Division
- 544th Grenadier Division (later 544th Volksgrenadier Division)
- 545th Grenadier Division (later 545th Volksgrenadier Division)
- 546th Grenadier Division
- 547th Grenadier Division (later 547th Volksgrenadier Division)
- 548th Grenadier Division (later 548th Volksgrenadier Division)
- 549th Grenadier Division (later 549th Volksgrenadier Division)
- 550th Grenadier Division
- 551st Grenadier Division (later 551st Volksgrenadier Division)
- 552nd Grenadier Division
- 553rd Grenadier Division (later 553rd Volksgrenadier Division)
- 558th Grenadier Division (later 558th Volksgrenadier Division)
- 559th Grenadier Division (later 559th Volksgrenadier Division)

560th Grenadier Division (later 560th Volksgrenadier Division)
561st Grenadier Division Ostpreußen 1 (later 561st Volksgrenadier Division)
562nd Grenadier Division Ostpreußen 2 (later 562nd Volksgrenadier Division)
563rd Grenadier Division (later 563rd Volksgrenadier Division)
564th Grenadier Division (later 564th Volksgrenadier Division)
565th Volksgrenadier Division
566th Volksgrenadier Division
567th Volksgrenadier Division
568th Volksgrenadier Division
569th Volksgrenadier Division
570th Volksgrenadier Division
571st Volksgrenadier Division
572nd Volksgrenadier Division
573rd Volksgrenadier Division
574th Volksgrenadier Division
575th Volksgrenadier Division
576th Volksgrenadier Division
577th Volksgrenadier Division
578th Volksgrenadier Division (previously 212th Infantry Division; later 212th Volksgrenadier Division)
579th Volksgrenadier Division
580th Volksgrenadier Division
581st Volksgrenadier Division
582nd Volksgrenadier Division
583rd Volksgrenadier Division
584th Volksgrenadier Division
585th Volksgrenadier Division
586th Volksgrenadier Division
587th Volksgrenadier Division
588th Volksgrenadier Division
702nd Static Infantry Division
708th Static Infantry Division (later 708th Coastal Defense Division, 708th Volksgrenadier Division)
709th Static Infantry Division
710th Static Infantry Division
716th Static Infantry Division (later 716th Volksgrenadier Division)
719th Infantry Division
999th Light Afrika Division

In addition to the Army's standard Jäger divisions were the units of the Gebirgsjäger divisions, which were initially outside the standard divisional numbering system. These mountain troops had their own series of numbers as follows:
1st Gebirgs Division
2nd Gebirgs Division
3rd Gebirgs Division
4th Gebirgs Division
5th Gebirgs Division
6th Gebirgs Division
7th Gebirgs Division
8th Gebirgs Division
9th Gebirgs Division

Gebirgs Korps of the Army:
XV Gebirgs Korps
XVIII Gebirgs Korps
XIX Gebirgs Korps
XXI Gebirgs Korps
XXII Gebirgs Korps
XXXVI Gebirgs Korps
XXXXIV Gebirgs Korps
LI Gebirgs Korps

However, it's worth noting that many of these Gebirgs Korps did not even feature any mountain troops within their ranks!

Infantry-Division neuer Art 1944

By March 1944 with the German Army more or less on the defensive a new type of infantry division saw its debut. Owing to strength problems and equipment shortages the new infantry division provided only two rifle battalions per regiment. The divisional reconnaissance battalion was converted to a fusilier battalion and was technically regarded as a seventh rifle battalion. While all these units were much smaller than the pre-1944 infantry divisions its firepower was increased, especially with the use of automatic weapons. There were also a variety of other weapons like the 3.7cm and 5cm Pak guns and mortars, which were supplied to the new infantry divisions to substitute the shortages of infantry guns. This helped the soldiers considerably especially when the majority of them were compelled to hold wider frontages against massive attacks.

Infantry Division 1945

In December 1944 the infantry division yet again went through a series of changes due to serious shortages of manpower and the lack of equipment. Not all the infantry divisions were reorganized as the majority were held on the front line bitterly fighting to stem the Red Army advance. The grenadier regiments still retained two battalions. These battalions had three rifle companies, which were equipped with four 7.5cm infantry guns and six 8cm mortars. The regiments' 13th heavy weapons company possessed two 15cm infantry guns and eight 12cm mortars, while the 14th Panzerjäger companies had 54 rocket-propelled launchers with another 18 of them in reserve. The primary use of the Panzerschrecks and Panzerfaust were to defend a well dug-in area and literally drench the vicinity with rocket fire, which in turn would hopefully halt the enemy.

Grenadiers

By 1943 grenadiers were organized as Panzergrenadier or Panzerjäger, and were removed from the standard line of infantry formations. The grenadier's role was principally responsible for supporting armour and was used to block armour with an anti-tank guns. However, as the war progressed and the need for manpower grew the grenadiers were often found fighting as normal infantry using a variety of weapons at their disposal. A typical grenadier regiment in 1944 consisted of the following:

Regimental Staff
Signal Platoon
Pioneer Platoon
Bicycle Platoon

Grenadier Battalion
Battalion Staff
Rifle Company
Company Troop
Rifle Group
Mortar Group
Company Train

Machine Gun Company
Machine Gun Platoon
Company Troop
Platoon Troop
Machine Gun Group
Mortar Platoon
Mortar Group
Company Train
Battalion Train

Infantry Gun Company
Company Troop
Heavy Infantry Gun Platoon
Light Infantry Gun Platoon
Company Train

Pak Company
Company Troop
Pak Platoon
Company Train

Light Infantry Column

Volksgrenadiers

The Volksgrenadier formations were created in late 1944, following the destruction of Army Group Centre during Operation Bagration. Due to the severe shortage of manpower and the need to create new infantry divisions the German Army drafted a number of personnel for defensive measures in the East. The Volksgrenadiers were normally formed out of anything the Replacement Army could find, which normally consisted of boys and elderly men, soldiers that were deemed physically unfit for service, those that had been wounded and were returning from hospitals, and transfers from the Kriegsmarine and Luftwaffe, usually organized around cadres of hardened veterans. The Volksgrenadiers were formed into divisions and consisted of six infantry battalions instead of the normal nine for infantry divisions. The name itself was intended to build morale, and was a way of inspiring nationalism of the people or Volk with older German military traditions of the grenadier. There were some 50 Volksgrenadier Divisions formed during the late war and a great number of these fought on the Eastern Front. However, the majority of the divisions were rushed into battle under-trained, and thus performed very badly, whilst some who acquitted themselves relatively well were too weak to avert the dire strategic situation in the East.

Party Militias

By late 1944 Hitler had no illusions about the desperate situation that Germany was facing. Manpower shortages were so great that even Hitler's generals began requesting the formation of a civilian defence militia, which could be grouped for defensive purposes, and help support the German Army in its role of trying to stem the Soviet advance. In October 1944 the Volkssturm or People's Home Guard were crated. All men capable of bearing arms in defence of the Fatherland between the ages of 16 and 60, and only those medically unfit to fight in the frontlines, were asked to flock to the recruiting stations all over Germany to enlist. The Volkssturm were not like the soldiers of the Home Guard units that were called-upon to defend England against a possible German invasion. Some Volkssturm were better armed in comparison, and some displayed a greater knowledge of battle tactics. Unlike the British Home Guard, the German Home Defence units were better trained in the art of tactical defence, and could be deadly adversaries to an advancing enemy tank. During training the new recruits familiarized themselves with Mauser rifles, Panzerfaust, and hand grenades that could be spared from dwindling army supplies.

Although the Volkssturm was not under German Army command out on the battlefield they fought alongside both the Waffen-SS and German Army. However, almost immediately the much-heralded Volkssturm proved incapable of being effective on the front lines in the East. Against the Russians it performed very poorly and constantly had to be stiffened by exhausted German Army troops.

Gebirgsjäger

The Gebirgsjäger or mountain troops were an elite group of soldiers under Army command and were trained to ski, climb, endure long marches, survive in appalling conditions and were given a role as crack shock troops. They were a light infantry group of well-trained soldiers. Each individual had to carry considerable personal kit in his rucksack, be he was also expected to scale mountains as well. The support elements that were available to traditional infantry divisions, such as armoured vehicles, tanks and artillery, were not supposed to be used by the Gebirgsjäger. Instead, they were supplied with weapons and other equipment that could be easily taken apart and carried by pack animals. However, by 1943 almost all Gebirgsjäger troops were no longer fighting in their natural element. Instead they were invariably utilised as assault infantry in conventional battles. Armoured vehicles, tanks and artillery, which had not been widely used were now supporting the mountain troops' survival across a wilderness of flat ground, for which they had never been initially trained for. By 1944, with the German Army desperately trying to hold its positions on the Eastern Front, the Gebirgsjäger were increasingly called upon to support the dwindling ranks of the infantry and to help fight a bitter retreat through Russia. The skill and willingness to hold back the enemy during the last desperate months of 1945 was fanatical. But as with the German infantry they fought alongside they could not maintain the vastly unequal struggle. Slowly and systematically they were ground down.

Luftwaffe Field Divisions

The Luftwaffe Field Divisions were first raised in 1942 and were technically regarded as a private army under the command of the Luftwaffe. Since 1941 the Luftwaffe's strength had grown to nearly 1,700,000 personnel, most of whom served in a non-flying capacity. In fact, on the Eastern Front anti-aircraft artillery had some 571,000 of the Luftwaffe's strength. Altogether, the Luftwaffe formed nearly a quarter of the German strength in Russia and it was deemed a considerable reservoir of trained men. It was not until the German Army had incurred its first major military setback in late 1941 that it decided to ask Reichsmarschall Herman Goring to raise the first Luftwaffe Field Divisions and help bolster the armies hard-pressed frontline units. On the Eastern Front the first Luftwaffe field divisions fought poorly and were totally unprepared for the shock of combat in Russia. As a consequence losses were high. Eventually, by late 1943 the Army, ever eager to stabilise the deteriorating situation, finally took control of the Luftwaffe field divisions. Almost immediately they were reorganized as Army divisions under the new 1944 infantry division establishment. For the last years of the war the Luftwaffe field divisions continued to serve relatively well in Russia after the transfer to the Army.

Panzer Divisions

The Panzer divisions were the backbone of the German Army. Not only did they support the infantry divisions' drive, but they also helped reduce the numbers of casualties sustained on the battlefield. However, within months of the invasion almost one-third of the Panzer divisions had been lost. By the end of 1941 tank strength was down by 50%, and there were less than 1,400 operational and damaged tanks that remained of the once powerful force. But despite the losses throughout 1942, the Germans began recreating and rebuilding all of the lost or depleted divisions by redirecting replacements in other theatres of war and adsorbing them into the Panzer divisions in Russia.

By the beginning of 1943 the problems continued to escalate, and out of the eight Panzer divisions that were totally annihilated, only four of them could be replaced. Despite the losses, the Germans were still determined as ever to pour all available resources into the armoured force of the Panzer divisions. Throughout the early cold months of 1943, the Panzerwaffe built up the strength of the badly depleted Panzer divisions. Although its divisions were still in a weakened condition, by June 1943 it fielded some 24 Panzer divisions on the Eastern Front alone. This was a staggering transformation of a Panzer force that had lost immeasurable amounts of armour in less than two years of combat. But the Panzerwaffe during the early summer was not the same as it had been during its victorious summer operations two years earlier. Although it fielded a relatively powerful armoured force, it was still understrength and could only be bolstered by newer and more potent armoured vehicles like the Panther, Sturmpanzer IV Brummbär, Panzerjäger IV Nashorn, and the Panzerjäger Elefant tank destroyer. It seemed a very impressive array of armour, but these vehicles were not only mechanically unreliable because they had been rushed to the Eastern Front too rapidly to fill the dwindling units, but there were too few of them to really make any averse change to the declining military situation in Russia.

Even so, they fought on under army command leadership hoping to stem the rout.

The following is a list of Panzer-Divisions under German Army command that fought on the Eastern Front between June 1943 until April 1945:

1.Panzer-Division

Units:

Panzer Regiment 1
Panzer Artillery Regiment 73
Panzergrenadier Regiments 1, 113
Panzer Aufklärungs-Abteilung (Reconnaissance Battalion) 1

APPENDIX III: ORGANISATION, UNIT LISTINGS

Theatres of Operation:

Ukraine November – December 1943
Hungary and Austria June 1944 – May 1945

2. Panzer-Division

Units:

Panzer Regiment 3
Panzergrenadier Regiments 2, 304
Panzer Artillery Regiment 74
Panzer Aufklärungs-Abteilung 2

Theatres of Operation:

Army Group Centre (Smolensk, Orel, Kiev) 1942 – 1943
France and W Germany 1944 – 1945

3. Panzer-Division

Units:

Panzer Regiment 6
Panzergrenadier Regiments 3, 394
Panzer Artillery Regiment 75
Panzer Aufklärungs-Abteilung 3

Theatres of Operation:

Southern Russia – Kharkov and Dnepr Bend 1943
Ukraine and Poland 1944
Hungary and Austria 1944 – 1945

4. Panzer-Division

Units:

Panzer Regiment 35
Panzergrenadier Regiment 12, 33
Panzer Artillery Regiment 103
Panzer Aufklärungs-Abteilung 4

Theatres of Operation:

Kursk 1943
Latvia 1944
West Prussia 1945

5. Panzer-Division

Units:

Panzer Regiment 31
Panzergrenadier Regiments 13, 14
Panzer Artillery Regiment 116
Panzer Aufklärungs-Abteilung 5

Theatres of Operation:

Central Russia – Kursk, Dnepr, Latvia, and Kurland 1941 – 1944
East Prussia 1944 – 45

6. Panzer-Division

Units:

Panzergrenadier Regiment 4, 114
Panzer Regiment 11
Panzer Artillery Regiment 76
Panzer Aufklärungs-Abteilung 6

Theatres of Operation:

Russia 1941 – 44
Hungary and Austria 1944 – 45

7. Panzer-Division

Units:

Panzer Regiment 25
Panzergrenadier Regiments 6,7
Panzer Artillery Regiment 78
Panzer Aufklärungs-Abteilung 7

Theatres of Operation:

Baltic Coast and Prussia 1944 – 45

8. Panzer-Division

Units:

Panzer Regiment 10
Panzergrenadier Regiments 8,28
Panzer Artillery Regiment 80
Panzer Aufklärungs-Abteilung 8

Theatres of Operation:

Kursk 1943
(Transferred To the West)

11. Panzer-Division

Units:

Panzer Regiment 15
Panzergrenadier Regiments 110,111

Panzer Artillery Regiment 119
Panzer Aufklärungs-Abteilung 11

Theatres of Operation:

Russia 1941 – 44 (Orel, Belgorod, Krivoi Rog and Korsun)
Transferred to Western Europe 1944

12.Panzer-Division

Units:

Panzer Regiment 29
Panzergrenadier Regiments 5,25
Panzer Artillery Regiment 2
Panzer Aufklärungs-Abteilung 12

Theatres of Operation:

Russia Army Group Centre 1941 – 1944
Orel and Middle Dnepr 1943
Kurland 1945

13.Panzer-Division

Units:

Panzer Regiment 4
Panzergrenadier Regiments 66,93
Panzer Artillery Regiment 13
Panzer Aufklärungs-Abteilung 13

Theatre of Operations:

Caucasus and the Kuban 1943 – 1944
Krivoi Rog 1944
Hungary 1944 – 1945
Destroyed and later reformed as Panzer Division 'Feldeherrnhalle' 2

16.Panzer-Division

Units:

Panzer Regiment 2
Panzergrenadier Regiments 64,79
Panzer Artillery Regiment 16
Panzer Aufklärungs-Abteilung 16

Theatres of Operation:

Russia – Kiev 1943
Poland 1944–45
Destroyed early 1945, reformed, serving in Silesia

17.Panzer-Division

Units:

Panzer Regiment 39
Panzergrenadier Regiments 40,63
Panzer Artillery Regiment 27
Panzer Aufklärungs-Abteilung 17

Theatres of Operation:

Russia (Central and Southern Sectors) 1941 – 1944
Poland, Silesia 1944–45

18.Panzer-Division

Units:

Panzer Regiment 18
Panzergrenadier Regiments 52,101
Panzer Artillery Regiment 88
Panzer Aufklärungs-Abteilung 8

Theatres of Operation:

Russian Central and Southern Sectors 1943
Later disbanded, elements being used to form the 18. Artillery Division

19.Panzer-Division

Units:

Panzer Regiment 27
Panzergrenadier Regiments 73,74
Panzer Artillery Regiment 19
Panzer Aufklärungs-Abteilung 19

Theatres of Operation:

Russian Central and Southern Sectors 1943 – 1944
Poland 1944
Silesia 1945

20.Panzer-Division

Panzer Regiment 21
Panzergrenadier Regiments 59,112
Panzer Artillery Regiment 92
Panzer Aufklärungs-Abteilung 20

Theatres of Operations:

Orel 1943
Rumania 1944
East Prussia 1944

Hungary 1944
Saxony 1945

21.Panzer-Division (second formation; the first destroyed in Tunisia 1943)

Units:

Panzer Regiment 22
Panzergrenadier Regiments 125,192
Panzer Artillery Regiment 155
Panzer Aufklärungs-Abteilung 21

Theatres of Operations:

Brandenburg, Berlin area 1945

23.Panzer-Division

Units:

Panzer Regiment 23
Panzergrenadier Regiments 126,128
Panzer Artillery Regiment 128
Panzer Aufklärungs-Abteilung 23

Theatres of Operation:

Caucasus 1943
Dnepr Bend 1944
Poland 1944 (refit)
Hungary 1945

24.Panzer-Division

Units:

Panzer Regiment 24
Panzergrenadier Regiments 21,26
Panzer Artillery Regiment 89
Panzer Aufklärungs-Abteilung 24

Theatres of Operation:

Kiev and Dnepr Bend 1943
Poland 1944
Hungary 1944
Slovakia 1944
East Prussia 1945

25.Panzer-Division

Units:

Panzer Regiment 9
Panzergrenadier Regiments 146,147
Panzer Artillery Regiment 91
Panzer Aufklärungs-Abteilung 25

Theatres of Operation:

Russia Southern sector 1943
Kiev 1943
Denmark 1944 (Refit)
Poland 1944
Silesia 1945

APPENDIX IV

German Order of Battle, Eastern Front July 1943

ARMY GROUP NORTH

Reserves:
388th Field Division
207th Security Division
281st Security Division
285th Security Division
18th Panzergrenadier Division
223rd Infantry Division

EIGHTEENTH ARMY

Reserves:
226th StuG Abteilung
912th StuG Abteilung
563rd Panzerjager Abteilung
121st Infantry Division
28th Jäger Division

XXXVIII Army Corps
1st Luftwaffe Field Division
717th Infantry Division
2nd SS.Infantry Brigade 'Latvian'

I Army Corps
13th Luftwaffe Field Division
227th Infantry Division

XXVIII Army Corps
96th Infantry Division
61st Infantry Division
81st Infantry Division
12th Luftwaffe Field Division
225th Infantry Division
132nd Infantry Division

XXVI Army Corps
212th Infantry Division
1st Infantry Division
11th Infantry Division
69th Infantry Division
290th Infantry Division
23rd Infantry Division
5th Gebirgsjäger Division

LIV Army Corps
21st Infantry Division
24th Infantry Division
254th Infantry Division
4th SS Panzergrenadier Police Division 'Polizei'
58th Infantry Division

L Army Corps
250th Spanish Infantry Division
170th Infantry Division
215th Infantry Division

III Luftwaffe Field Corps
9th Luftwaffe Field Division
10th Luftwaffe Field Division

SIXTEENTH ARMY

Reserves:
184th StuG Abteilung
9th Luftwaffe Field Division
69th Infantry Division

II Army Corps
331st Infantry Division
12th Infantry Division
218th Infantry Division
123rd Infantry Division
93rd Infantry Division

Group 'Hohne' Army Corps
21st Luftwaffe Field Division
122nd Infantry Division
32nd Infantry Division

X Army Corps
5th Jäger Division
30th Infantry Division
8th Jäger Division
126th Infantry Division
329th Infantry Division

ARMY GROUP CENTRE

Reserves:
190th StuG Abteilung
600th StuG Abteilung
5th Panzer Division
8th Panzer Division
83rd Infantry Division
36th Infantry Division
390th Field Division
391st Field Division

Group 'Esebeck'
10th Panzergrenadier Division
12th Panzer Division
4th Panzer Division
286th Security Division
221st Security Division
203rd Security Division

VII Hungarian Corps
201st Hungarian Light Division
8th Hungarian Light Division
2nd Hungarian Light Division
5th Hungarian Light Division

THIRD PANZER ARMY

Reserves:
201st Security Division

VI Army Corps
206th Infantry Division
330th Infantry Division
87th Infantry Division

II Luftwaffe Field Corps
4th Luftwaffe Field Division
3rd Luftwaffe Field Division
6th Luftwaffe Field Division
2nd Luftwaffe Field Division

LIX Army Corps
263rd Infantry Division
291st Infantry Division

XXXXIII Army Corps
20th Panzergrenadier Division
205th Infantry Division

FOURTH ARMY

Reserves:
667th StuG Abteilung
183rd Infantry Division
253rd Infantry Division

LVI Panzer Corps
131st Infantry Division
14th Infantry Division
321st Infantry Division

XII Army Corps
267th Infantry Division
260th Infantry Division
268th Infantry Division

IX Army Corps
342nd Infantry Division
252nd Infantry Division
35th Infantry Division

XXXIX Army Corps
337th Infantry Division
95th Infantry Division
129th Infantry Division

XXVII Army Corps
246th Infantry Division
197th Infantry Division
256th Infantry Division
52nd Infantry Division

SECOND PANZER ARMY

Reserves:
202nd StuG Abteilung
270th StuG Abteilung
112th Infantry Division
707th Infantry Division

LV Army Corps
339th Infantry Division
110th Infantry Division
296th Infantry Division
134th Infantry Division

LIII Army Corps
211th Infantry Division
293rd Infantry Division
25th Panzergrenadier Division
208th Infantry Division
221st Security Division

XXXV Army Corps
34th Infantry Division
56th Infantry Division
262nd Infantry Division
299th Infantry Division

NINTH ARMY

Reserves:

561st Panzerjäger Abteilung
299th Infantry Division
36th Infantry Division

XXIII Army Corps

185th StuG Abteilung
189th StuG Abteilung
36th Infantry Division
383rd Infantry Division
216th Infantry Division
78th Sturm Division

XXXXI Panzer Corps

656th Panzerjäger Regiment
653rd Panzerjager Abteilung
654th Panzerjäger Abteilung
216th Storm Panzer Abteilung
86th Infantry Division
292nd Infantry Division
18th Panzer Division

XXXXVII Panzer Corps

245th StuG Abteilung
904th StuG Abteilung
21st Panzer Brigade (included 505th sPz Abteilung, Tigers)
2nd Panzer Division
6th Infantry Division
20th Panzer Division
9th Panzer Division

XXXXVI Panzer Corps

909th StuG Abteilung
177th StuG Abteilung
244th StuG Abteilung
31st Infantry Division
7th Infantry Division
258th Infantry Division
102nd Infantry Division

XX Army Corps

72nd Infantry Division
45th Infantry Division
137th Infantry Division
251st Infantry Division

SECOND ARMY

Reserves:

1st Hungarian Light Division

XIII Army Corps

559th Panzerjäger Abteilung
82nd Infantry Division
340th Infantry Division
377th Infantry Division
327th Infantry Division

VII Army Corps

616th Panzerjäger Abteilung
26th Infantry Division
323rd Infantry Division
75th Infantry Division
68th Infantry Division
88th Infantry Division

ARMY GROUP SOUTH

Reserves:

24th Hungarian Light Division
213th Security Division
454th Security Division
444th Security Division
24th Rumanian Infantry Division

LXII Reserve Corps

143rd Reserve Division
147th Reserve Division

FOURTH PANZER ARMY

LII Army Corps

57th Infantry Division
255th Infantry Division
332nd Infantry Division

XXXXVIII Panzer Corps

51st Panzer Abteilung
52nd Panzer Abteilung
911th StuG Abteilung
616th Flak Battalion
3rd Panzer Division
11th Panzer Division
167th Infantry Division
Grossdeutschland Panzergrenadier Division

II SS Panzer Corps

1st SS Panzergrenadier Division
2nd SS Panzergrenadier Division
3rd SS Panzergrenadier Division
167th Infantry Division

ARMY 'KEMPF'

XXXXII Army Corps

560th Panzerjäger Abteilung

663rd Panzerjäger Abteilung
77th Luftwaffe Flak Regiment
161st Infantry Division
282nd Infantry Division
39th Infantry Division

XI Army Corps

393rd StuG Battery
905th StuG Abteilung
4th Luftwaffe Flak Regiment
7th Luftwaffe Flak Regiment
48th Luftwaffe Flak Regiment
320th Infantry Division
106th Infantry Division

III Panzer Corps

228th StuG Abteilung
503rd Tiger Panzer Abteilung
99th Luftwaffe Flak Regiment
153rd Luftwaffe Flak Regiment
6th Panzer Division
7th Panzer Division
19th Panzer Division
168th Infantry Division

FIRST PANZER ARMY

XXIV Panzer Corps

23rd Panzer Division
17th Panzer Division
5th SS Panzergrenadier Division

XXX Army Corps

62nd Infantry Division
38th Infantry Division
387th Infantry Division

XXXX Panzer Corps

333rd Infantry Division
46th Infantry Division
257th Infantry Division

LVII Panzer Corps

15th Infantry Division
198th Infantry Division
328th Infantry Division

SIXTH ARMY

Reserves:

209th StuG Abteilung
210th StuG Abteilung
243rd StuG Abteilung
16th Panzergrenadier Division

XXIX Army Corps

16th Panzergrenadier Division
15th Luftwaffe Field Division
17th Infantry Division
336th Infantry Division

XVII Army Corps

294th Infantry Division
306th Infantry Division
302nd Infantry Division

IV Army Corps

304th Infantry Division
335th Infantry Division
3rd Gebirgsjäger Division

ARMY GROUP 'A'

Reserves:

13th Panzer Division
4th Rumanian Mountain Division
5th Luftwaffe Field Division

Crimea Sector:

153rd Field Division
13th Panzer Division
355th Infantry Division
381st Field Division

Reserves:

1st Slovakian Motorized Division
Rumanian Mountain Corps:
4th Rumanian Mountain Division
2nd Rumanian Mountain Division

SEVENTEENTH ARMY

Reserves:

191st StuG Abteilung
249th StuG Abteilung

Group 'Allmendinger'

9th Infantry Division
1st Rumanian Mountain Division

Rumanian Cavalry Corps

9th Rumanian Cavalry Division
19th Rumanian Infantry Division

Group 'Kness'

6th Rumanian Cavalry Division
4th Gebirgsjäger Division

Group 'von Bunau'

1st Rumanian Mountain Division

73rd Infantry Division

XXXXIV Army Corps

97th Jäger Division
79th Infantry Division
101st Jäger Division
19th Rumanian Infantry Division
79th Infantry Division
3rd Rumanian Mountain Division
10th Rumanian Infantry Division
98th Infantry Division
125th Infantry Division

XXXXIX Gebirgs Corps

370th Infantry Division
50th Infantry Division
125th Infantry Division
3rd Rumanian Mountain Division
10th Rumanian Infantry Division
13th Panzer Division

APPENDIX V

German Order of Battle, Eastern Front, 15 June 1944

ARMY GROUP NORTH

Reserves:

Field Division 'Nord'
12th Panzer Division

SIXTEENTH ARMY

Reserves:

24th Infantry Division
69th Infantry Division
281st Security Division
285th Security Division

I Army Corps

205th Infantry Division
87th Infantry Division

X Army Corps

389th Infantry Division
290th Infantry Division
263rd Infantry Division

II Army Corps

81st Infantry Division
329th Infantry Division
23rd Infantry Division

VI SS-Corps

15th SS.Grenadier Division 'Latvian 1'
19th SS.Grenadier Division 'Latvian 2'
93rd Infantry Division

L Army Corps

218th Infantry Division
132nd Infantry Division
83rd Infantry Division

EIGHTEENTH ARMY

Reserves:

215th Infantry Division

XXXVIII Army Corps

21st Luftwaffe Field Division
32nd Infantry Division
121st Infantry Division

XXVIII Army Corps

30th Infantry Division
21st Infantry Division
212th Infantry Division
126th Infantry Division
12th Luftwaffe Field Division
1st Estonian Border Security Regiment
207th Security Division

ARMY 'NARVA'

Army Reserves:

61st Infantry Division

XXVI Army Corps

227th Infantry Division
170th Infantry Division
225th Infantry Division

XXXXIII Army Corps

58th Infantry Division
11th Infantry Division
122nd Infantry Division

III SS Panzer Corps

11th SS Panzergrenadier Division 'Nordland'
20th SS Grenadier Division 'Estonian 1'
Kustenverteidigung 'Ost'
Luftwaffe Flak Division 'Estonian'
Kustenverteidigung 'West'
285th Security Division 'Estonia'

ARMY GROUP CENTRE

Reserves:

707th Infantry Division
14th Infantry Division

OKH Reserves:

Panzer Group 'F'
221st Security Division
391st Security Division

SECOND ARMY

Reserves:

5th Hungarian Reserve Division
23rd Hungarian Reserve Division
4th Kavallerie Brigade
1st Hungarian Cavalry Division

VIII Army Corps

5th Jäger Division
211th Infantry Division
12th Hungarian Reserve Division

XX Army Corps

3 Kavallerie Brigade

XXIII Army Corps

7th Infantry Division
203rd Security Division

NINTH ARMY

LV Army Corps

102nd Infantry Division
292nd Infantry Division

XXXXI Panzer Corps

129th Infantry Division
35th Infantry Division
36th Infantry Division

XXXV Army Corps

45th Infantry Division
383rd Infantry Division
6th Infantry Division
296th Infantry Division
134th Infantry Division
129th Infantry Division

FOURTH ARMY

Reserves:

286th Security Division

XII Army Corps

57th Infantry Division
267th Infantry Division
18th Panzergrenadier Division

XXXIX Panzer Corps

31st Infantry Division
12th Infantry Division
337th Infantry Division
110th Infantry Division

XXVII Army Corps

260th Infantry Division
25th Panzergrenadier Division
78th Sturm Division

THIRD PANZER ARMY

Reserves:

201st Security Division
95th Infantry Division

VI Army Corps

256th Infantry Division
299th Infantry Division
197th Infantry Division

LIII Army Corps

206th Infantry Division
6th Luftwaffe Field Division
4th Luftwaffe Field Division
246th Infantry Division

IX Army Corps

Division Group '252'

ARMY GROUP 'NORTH UKRAINE'

Reserves:

II SS Panzer Corps
9th SS Panzer Division 'Hohenstaufen'
10th SS Panzer Division 'Frundsberg'
16th SS Panzer Division 'Reichsführer SS'

FIRST HUNGARIAN ARMY

Army Reserves:

2nd Hungarian Panzer Division
19th Hungarian Reserve Division

VI Hungarian Corps

2nd Hungarian Mountain Brigade
Brigade 'Schlebrugge'
27th Hungarian Light Division
1st Hungarian Mountain Brigade

XI Army Corps

18th Hungarian Reserve Division

25th Hungarian Infantry Division
101st Jäger Division
24th Hungarian Infantry Division

VII Hungarian Corps

68th Infantry Division
16th Hungarian Infantry Division

FIRST PANZER ARMY

Reserves:

III Panzer Corps
1st Panzer Division
7th Panzer Division
8th Panzer Division
17th Panzer Division
20th Panzergrenadier Division

XXXXVI Panzer Corps

367th Infantry Division
168th Infantry Division
1st Infantry Division

LIX Army Corps

20th Hungarian Infantry Division
208th Infantry Division
254th Infantry Division

XXIV Panzer Corps

371st Infantry Division
75th Infantry Division
100th Jäger Division

XXXXVIII Panzer Corps

359th Infantry Division
96th Infantry Division
357th Infantry Division
349th Infantry Division

FOURTH PANZER ARMY

Reserves:

454th Security Division
4th Panzer Division
5th Panzer Division
28th Jäger Division

XIII Army Corps

361st Infantry Division
340th Infantry Division

XXXXII z.b.V. Corps

291st Infantry Division
88th Infantry Division
72nd Infantry Division

214th Infantry Division

LVI Panzer Corps

1st Ski Jäger Division
253rd Infantry Division
131st Infantry Division
342nd Infantry Division
26th Infantry Division

ARMY GROUP 'SOUTH UKRAINE'

V Army Corps

XXXXIX Gebirgs Corps

153rd Field Division
1st Slovakian Infantry Division
8th Rumanian Cavalry Division
1st Rumanian Army Division

ARMY GROUP 'DUMITRESCU'

Reserves:

LXXII z.b.V. Corps

THIRD RUMANIAN ARMY

Army Reserves:

9th Rumanian Infantry Division

III Rumanian Corps

110th Rumanian Infantry Brigade
2nd Rumanian Infantry Division
15th Rumanian Infantry Division
685th z.b.V. Regiment

XXIX Army Corps

304th Infantry Division
21st Rumanian Infantry Division
4th Rumanian Mountain Division
9th Infantry Division

SIXTH ARMY

Reserves:

3rd Panzer Division
13th Panzer Division

XXX Army Corps

306th Infantry Division
15th Infantry Division
257th Infantry Division
302nd Infantry Division
384th Infantry Division

LII Army Corps

17th Infantry Division
320th Infantry Division
97th Jäger Division
294th Infantry Division
4th Gebirgsjäger Division

XXXXIV Army Corps

335th Infantry Division
282nd Infantry Division
10th Panzergrenadier Division
258th Infantry Division

VII Army Corps

14th Rumanian Infantry Division
106th Infantry Division
370th Infantry Division

ARMY GROUP 'WOHLER'

Reserves:

XXXX Panzer Corps

18th Rumanian Mountain Division

EIGHTH ARMY

IV Rumanian Corps

102nd Rumanian Mountain Brigade
5th Rumanian Cavalry Division

IV Army Corps

376th Infantry Division
11th Rumanian Infantry Division
23rd Panzer Division
79th Infantry Division
3rd Rumanian Infantry Division

FOURTH RUMANIAN ARMY

Army Reserves:

1st Rumanian Cavalry Division
24th Panzer Division
3rd SS Panzer Division 'Totenkopf'
8th Rumanian Infantry Division
198th Infantry Division

LVII Panzer Corps

Reserves:

14th Panzer Division

VI Rumanian Corps

7th Rumanian Infantry Division
76th Infantry Division
18th Rumanian Mountain Division
5th Rumanian Infantry Division
101st Rumanian Mountain Brigade

V Rumanian Corps

4th Rumanian Infantry Division
1st Rumanian Guard Division

LVII Panzer Corps

1st Rumanian Infantry Division
46th Infantry Division
13th Rumanian Infantry Division

I Rumanian Corps

6th Rumanian Infantry Division
20th Rumanian Infantry Division

VII Army Corps

104th Rumanian Infantry Brigade
103rd Rumanian Infantry Brigade

XVII Army Corps

3rd Gebirgsjäger Division
8th Jäger Division

APPENDIX VI

German Order of Battle, Berlin, 12–26 April 1945

OKW RESERVE (LVI Panzer Corps, 9th Army)

18th Panzergrenadier Division
Commander: General Josef Rauch

30th & 51st Panzergrenadier Regts
118th Panzer Regt
18th Artillery Regt

ARMY GROUP 'VISTULA'

Commander: Gen Gotthard Heinrici

III SS 'Germanic' Panzer Corps

Commander: SS Gen Felix Steiner

11th SS 'Nordland' Panzergrenadier Division (some units served independently, and are listed below)
23rd 'Norge' Panzergrenadier Regiment
24th 'Danmark' Panzergrenadier Regiment
11th SS 'Hermann von Salza' Panzer Battalion
503rd SS Heavy Tank Battalion
11th SS 'Nordland' Armoured Reconnaissance Battalion
23rd SS 'Nederland' Panzergrenadier Division
27th SS 'Langemarck' Grenadier Division
28th SS 'Wallonien' Grenadier Division

THIRD PANZER ARMY

Commander: General Hasso von Manteuffel

'Swinemunde' Corps

Commander: General Ansat

402nd & 2nd Naval Divisions

XXXII Corps

Commander: General Schack

'Voigt' & 281st Infantry Divisions
549th Volksgrenadier Division
Stettin Garrison

'Oder' Corps

SS General von dem Bach – General Hörnlein

610th & 'Klossek' Infantry Divisions

XXXXVI Panzer Corps

Commander: General Martin Gareis

547th Volksgrenadier Division
1st Naval Division

NINTH ARMY

Commander: General Theodor Busse

156th Infantry Division
541st Volksgrenadier Division
404th Volksgrenadier-Artillery-Corps
406th Volksgrenadier-Artillery-Corps
408th Volksgrenadier-Artillery-Corps

CI Corps

Commander: General Wilhelm Berlin / General Friedrich Sixt

5th Light Infantry Division
606th Infantry Division
309th 'Berlin' Infantry Division
25th Panzergrenadier Division
111th SPG Training Battalion
'1001 Nights' Combat Group

LVI Panzer Corps

Commander: General Helmuth Weidling

9th Fallschirmjäger Division
25th, 26th & 27th Fallschirmjäger Regiment
9th Fallschirmjäger Artillery Regiment
20th Panzergrenadier Division
76th & 90th Panzergrenadier Regiment
8th Panzer Battalion
20th Artillery Regt

'Müncheberg' Panzer Division
Commander: General Werner Mummert

1st & 2nd 'Müncheberg' Panzergrenadier Regts
'Müncheberg' Panzer Regiment
'Müncheberg' Armoured Artillery Regiment
920th SPG Training Battalion

XI SS Panzer Corps

Commander: SS General Mathias Kleinheisterkamp

303rd 'Döberitz' Infantry Division
169th Infantry Division
712th Infantry Division
'Kurmark' Panzergrenadier Division
502nd SS Heavy Tank Battalion

Frankfurt an der Oder Garrison

Commander: General Ernst Biehler

V SS Mountain Corps

Commander: SS General Friedrich Jackeln

286th Infantry Division
32nd SS '30. Januar' Volksgrenadier Division
391st Sy Division
561st SS Tank Hunting Battalion

ARMY GROUP CENTRE

Commander: Field Marshal Ferdinand Schörner

FOURTH PANZER ARMY

Commander: General Fritz-Herbert Gräser

V Corps

Commander: General Wagner

35th SS Police Grenadier Division
36th SS Grenadier Division
275th Infantry Division
342nd Infantry Division
21st Panzer Division

TWELFTH ARMY

Commander: General Walter Wenck

XX Corps

Commander: General Carl-Erik Koehler

'Theodor Körner' RAD Division
'Ulrich von Hutten' Infantry Division
'Ferdinand von Schill' Infantry Division
'Scharnhorst' Infantry Division

Prior to the final battle of Berlin between 12 and 21 April 1945 OKW hastily formed the following German Army formations for the final battle around Berlin:

XXXIX Panzer Corps

Commander: General Karl Arndt

'Clausewitz' Panzer Division
'Schlageter' RAD Division
84th Infantry Division

During the final battle of Berlin between 21 and 26 April 1945 OKW hastily formed the following German Army, Waffen-SS and Luftwaffe field formations:
'Clausewitz' Panzer Division
84th Infantry Division
'Hamburg' Reserve Infantry Division
'Meyer' Infantry Division

XXXXI Panzer Corps

Commander: General Holste

'von Hake' Infantry Division
199th Infantry Division
'V-Weapons' Infantry Division
1st HJ Tank Destroyer Brigade
'Hermann Göring' Jagdpanzer Brigade

XXXXVIII Panzer Corps

General Maximillian Reichsherr von Edelscheim

14th Flak Division
'Leipzig' Battle Group
'Halle' Battle Group

APPENDIX VII

German Army Ranks

German Army	Waffen-SS	British Army
Gemeiner, Landser	Schütze	Private
	Oberschütze	
Grenadier	Sturmmann	Lance Corporal
Obergrenadier		
Gefreiter	Rottenführer	Corporal
Obergefreiter	Unterscharführer	
Stabsgefreiter		
Unteroffizier	Scharführer	Sergeant
Unterfeldwebel	Oberscharführer	Colour Sergeant
Feldwebel		
Oberfeldwebel	Hauptscharführer	Sergeant Major
Stabsfeldwebel	Hauptbereitschaftsleiter	
	Sturmscharführer	Warrant Officer
Leutnant	Untersturmführer	Second Lieutenant
Oberleutnant	Obersturmführer	First Lieutenant
Hauptmann	Hauptsturmführer	Captain
Major	Sturmbannführer	Major
Oberstleutnant	Obersturmbannführer	Lieutenant Colonel
Oberst	Standartenführer	Colonel
	Oberführer	Brigadier General
Generalmajor	Brigadeführer	Major General
Generalleutnant	Gruppenführer	Lieutenant General
General	Obergruppenführer	General
Generaloberst	Oberstgruppenführer	
Generalfeldmarschall	Reichsführer-SS	

Bibliography

Part I

Documents

Kursk Order of Battle July 1943
Militärarchiv Freiburg/ Kursk/RHN68/K 9
Ost-Dokumentation. 10 Nr.Opr. XI. C/4
Bundesarchiv Koblenz
Oberkommando der Wehrmacht (OKW). Washington: National Archives Section, Microcopy Roll T–77 [OKW/T–77]

Published material

Choltitz, General von *Soldaten unter Soldaten.* Zurich, 1951
Engelmann, Joachim *Zitadelle: Die grosste Panzerschlacht im Osten 1943.* Friedberg, 1980
Gräser, Gerhard *Zwischen Kattegat und Kaukasus: Weg und Kampf der 198. Infanterie Division, 1939 – 1945.* Tübingen, 1961
Guderian, General Heinz *Erinnerungen eines Soldaten* Heidelberg, 1951
Heinrici, Gotthard "Zitadelle", *Wehrwissenschaftliche Rundschau*, 15
Hubatsch, Dr. Walther *Hitler's weisungen für der kriegführer, 1939 – 1945.* Frankfurt, 1962
Knobelsdorff, Otto von *Geschichte der niedersachsichen 19.Panzer division.* Bad Nauheim, 1958
Manstein, Field Marshal E.von *Verlorene siege.* Bonn, 1955
Mitteldorf, E. "Zitadelle", *Wehrwissenschaftliche Rundschau*, 1953
Paul, Wolfgang *Brennpunkte: Die Geschichte der 6.Panzer division 1937 – 1945.* Krefeld, 1977
Sieger, Fritz Freiherr von *Die Hohern dienststellen der Deutschen Wehrmacht, 1933 – 45.* Munich, 1953
Tessin, G. *Verbaende und Truppen der deutsch. Wehrmacht und Waffen-SS, 1939 – 1945.* Osnabrück, 1967–98

Part II

Documents

National Archives Microcopy T312, Records of German Field Commands, Armies: Armeeoberkommando 8 (Reels 54, 64, 66).
National Archives: Microcopy T–313, Records of German Field Commands, Panzer Armies and Waffen-SS.
National Archives: Microcopy 314, Records of Waffen-SS/Wehrmacht Armee-Korps, Field commands and II.Armee-Korps (Reels 131, 132, 133)
Battle Report Strengths and Orders: Bundesarchiv Koblenz. BA-K121 A/L.1

Published material

Buhlmann, G. *Die Vesorgung Fremder Heere.* Frauenfeld,1949
Grossmann, H. *Geschichte der 6. Infanterie Division.* Bad Nauheim, 1958
Kern, E. *General von Pannwitz und seine Kosaken.* Pr Oldendorf, 1971
Middeldorf, E. *Taktik Im Russlandfeldzug.* Darmstadt, 1956
Phillipi, A.G. & F. Heise *Der Feldzug gegen Sowjet Russland.* Kohlhammer, 1962
Piekalkiewicz, J. *Pferd und Reiter im Zweiten* Weltkieg. Munich, 1977
Tessin, G. *Verbaende und Truppen der deutsch. Wehrmacht und Waffen-SS, 1939–1945.* Osnabrück, 1967–98
Various authors *Die Wehrmacht im Kampf* (Series) Vols.3, 4, 7, 8, 11, 14, 15, 20.

Part III

Published material

Anon. *Die Kampfe um die Befeiung der Lausitz: wahrend der grossen Schlacht um Berlin, 1945.* Bautzen, 1975
Haupt, W. *Berlin 1945: Hitler's letzte Schlacht.* Rastatt, 1963
Lemke, T. *Alliierte Militarfahzeuge im Berlin 1945–1994,* Basdorf, 1996

Neufeldt, Hans-Joachim, Jurgen Huck & Georg Tessin *Zur Geschichte der Ordnungspolizei 1936–1945*. Koblenz, 1957

Schmidt-Richberg, E. *Der Endkampf auf dem Balkan*. Heidelberg, 1955

Schultz-Naumann, J. *The Last 30 Days: War Diary of the German Armed Forces High Command April to May 1945*. New York, 1991

Steiner, Felix *Die Freiwilligen: Idee and Opfergang*. Göttingen, 1958

Various authors *Die Wehrmacht im Kampf* (Series) Vols. 3, 4, 7, 8, 11, 14, 15, 20.

Also available from Helion & Company

For Europe
The French Volunteers of the Waffen-SS
Robert Forbes
528pp., circa 6 maps, 7 photos
Hardback   ISBN 978-1-874622-68-0

To the Bitter End
The Final Battles of Army Groups North Ukraine,
A, Centre, Eastern Front 1944–45
Rolf Hinze
232pp., 30 b/w photos, 30 maps
Hardback   ISBN 978-1-874622-36-9

Into the Abyss
The Last Years of the Waffen SS,
a Photographic History 1943–45
Ian Baxter
160pp., 190 photos, maps
Hardback   ISBN 978-1-874622-59-8

A SELECTION OF FORTHCOMING TITLES

Panzer Lehr Division 1944–45 (Helion WWII German Military Studies volume 1)
edited by Fred Steinhardt   ISBN 978-1-874622-28-4

Under Himmler's Command: The Personal Recollections of Oberst Hans-Georg Eismann,
Operations Officer, Army Group Vistula, Eastern Front 1945
Hans-Georg Eismann, edited by Fred Steinhardt   ISBN 978-1-874622-43-7

In the Fire of the Eastern Front: The Experiences of a Dutch Waffen-SS Volunteer
on the Eastern Front 1941–45
Hendrick C. Verton   ISBN 978-1-874622-54-3

HELION & COMPANY

26 Willow Road, Solihull, West Midlands, B91 1UE, England
Tel 0121 705 3393   Fax 0121 711 4075
Email: publishing@helion.co.uk Website: http://www.helion.co.uk

RECEIVED NOV 2 8 2007 5995